# A-Z BRACKNELL

G000136584

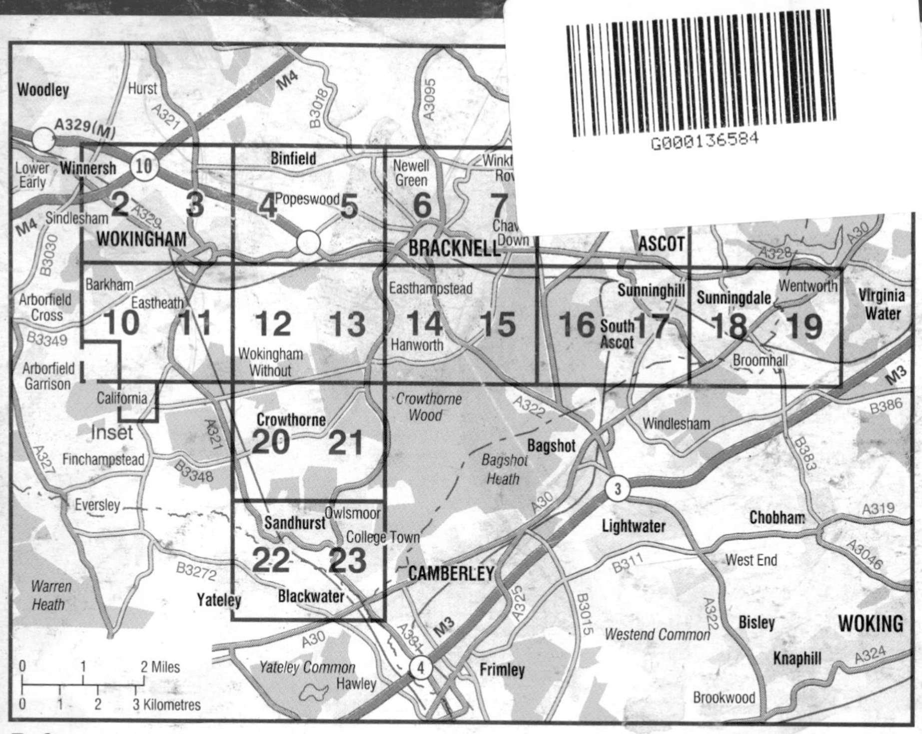


## Reference

| | |
|---|---|
| Motorway | M3 |
| A Road | A330 |
| Proposed | |
| B Road | B3430 |
| Dual Carriageway | |
| One Way Street<br>Traffic flow on A Roads is also indicated by a heavy line on the drivers left | |
| Pedestrianized Road | |
| Restricted Access | |
| Track | |
| Footpath | |
| Residential Walkway | |
| Railway | Level Crossing / Station |
| Built Up Area | |
| Local Authority Boundary | |
| Posttown Boundary | |
| Postcode Boundary within Posttown | |
| Map Continuation | 8 |
| Car Park selected | P |
| Church or Chapel | † |
| Fire Station | ■ |
| Hospital | H |
| House Numbers A & B Roads only | 79 24 |
| Information Centre | i |
| National Grid Reference | 485 |
| Police Station | ▲ |
| Post Office | ★ |
| Toilet | |
| with Facilities for the Disabled | |

**Scale** 1:15,840
4 inches to 1 mile

0 ¼ ½ ¾ Mile
0 250 500 750 Metres 1 Kilometre


**Copyright of Geographers' A-Z Map Company Limited**

Head Office : Fairfield Road, Borough Green, Sevenoaks, Kent TN15 8PP Tel: 01732 781000
Showrooms : 44 Gray's Inn Road, London WC1X 8HX Tel: 0171 242 9246

2
Twyford
RG10
Winnersh
Merryhill Green
Playing Field
The Forest Secondary School
Winnersh Prim. Sch.
Bentley Lane Piggeries
Depot
Caravan Site
Emm Brook
Junction 10
Toutley Bridge
Superstore
Club
M4 MOTORWAY
M4
A329(M)
A329
Furze Covert
Sports Field
Emmbrook Jun.& Inf. Schs.
Bearwood Prim. Sch.
Home Farm
Home Farm Bungalows
Home Farm Lodge
Church Lodge
ROYAL MERCHANT NAVY SCHOOL (BEARWOOD COLLEGE)
Electricity Control Centre
Bob's Copse
Poulter's Lodge
Football Grd.
The Hawthorns Prim. Sch.
Windmill Pond
Woosehill Centre
Woose Hill
Adult Training Cen.
Round Hill
Wokingham
10

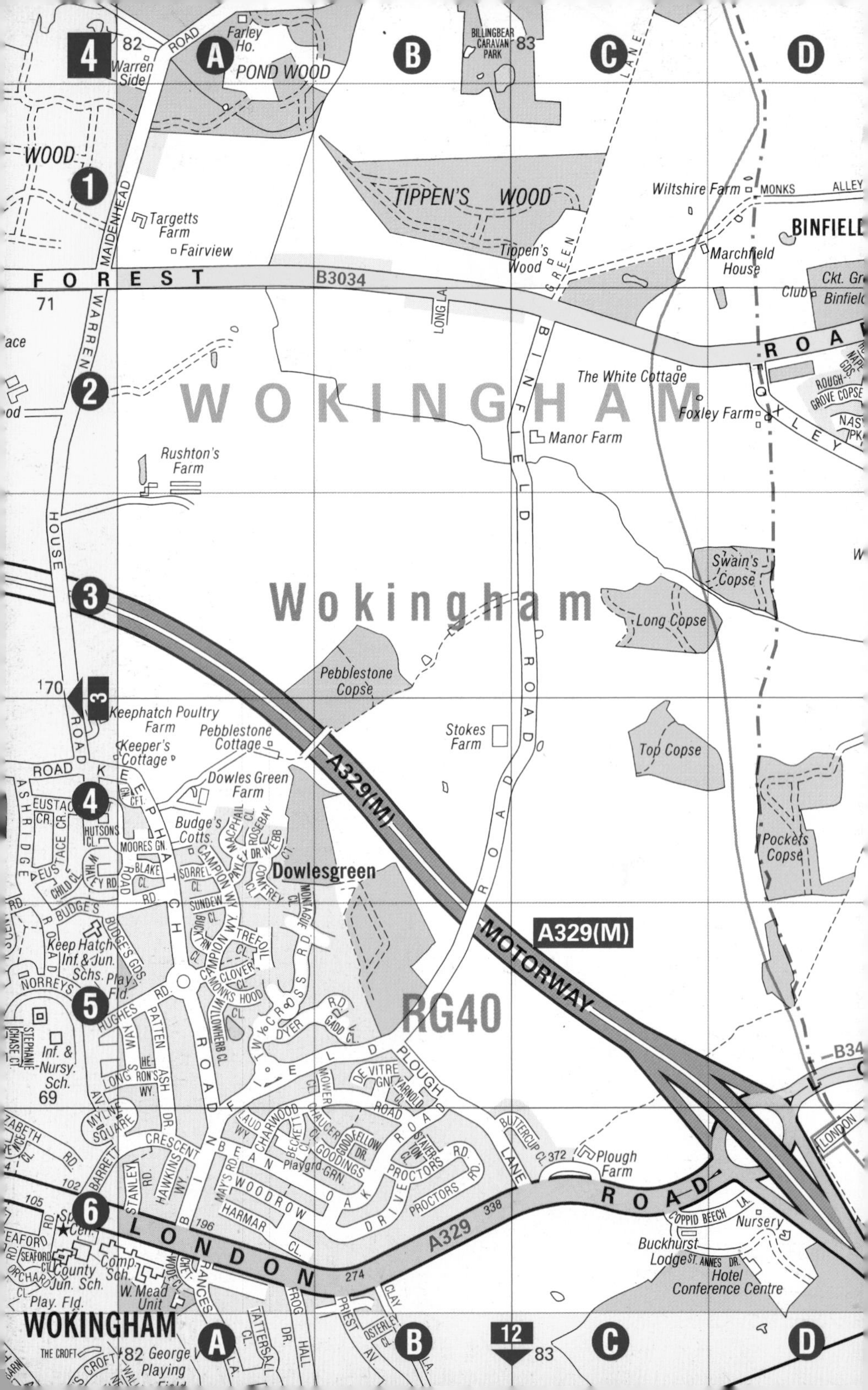
4
A
B
C
D
Farley Ho.
POND WOOD
Warren Side
BILLINGBEAR CARAVAN PARK
WOOD
TIPPEN'S WOOD
Targetts Farm
Fairview
Tippen's Wood
Wiltshire Farm
MONKS ALLEY
BINFIELD
Marchfield House
FOREST
B3034
ROAD
LONG LA.
GREEN LANE
MAIDENHEAD
Club
The White Cottage
Foxley Farm
FOXLEY
WOKINGHAM
Manor Farm
BINFIELD ROAD
Rushton's Farm
HOUSE
WARREN
Swain's Copse
Wokingham
Long Copse
Pebblestone Copse
Keephatch Poultry Farm
Pebblestone Cottage
Keeper's Cottage
Stokes Farm
Top Copse
Dowles Green Farm
A329(M)
Pockets Copse
Budge's Cotts.
Dowlesgreen
KEEPHATCH ROAD
MOTORWAY
Keep Hatch Inf. & Jun. Schs.
Play. Fld.
RG40
Inf. & Nursy. Sch.
PLOUGH LANE
Plough Farm
BUTTERCUP CL.
LONDON ROAD
A329
COPPID BEECH LA.
Nursery
Buckhurst Lodge
Hotel Conference Centre
County Jun. Sch.
Comp. Sch.
W. Mead Unit
Play. Fld.
WOKINGHAM
George V Playing Field
12
83

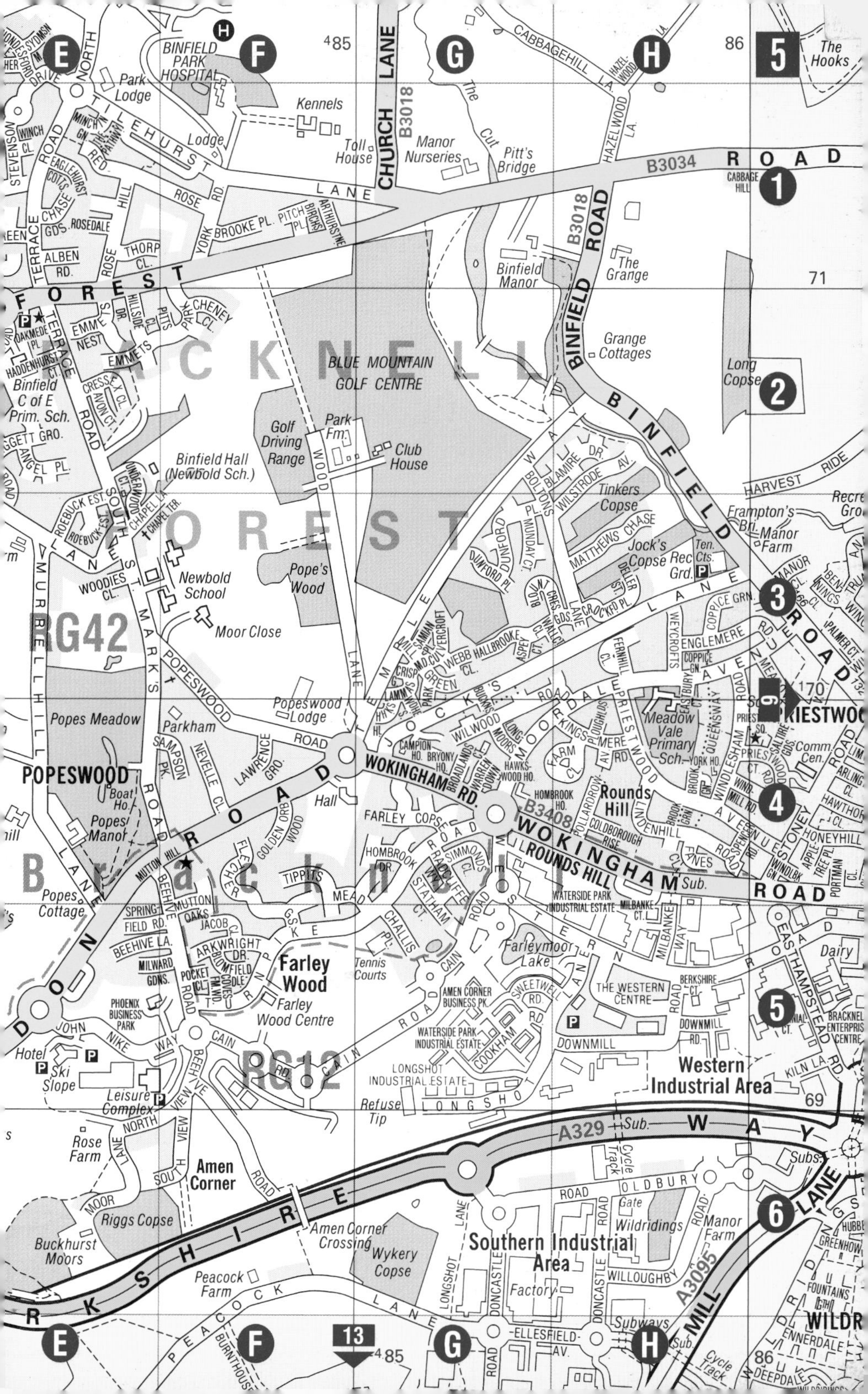
E
F
G
H
485
86
5
The Hooks
BINFIELD PARK HOSPITAL
Park Lodge
Kennels
CHURCH LANE
B3018
Toll House
Manor Nurseries
The Cut
Pitt's Bridge
CABBAGEHILL LA.
HAZELWOOD LA.
B3034
ROAD
CABBAGE HILL
1
TILEHURST LANE
Lodge
ROSE RD.
BROOKE PL.
PITCH PL.
BIRCHS
ARTHURSTONE
STEVENSON
WINCH CL.
EAGLEHURST
COTTS CHASE GDS.
ROSEDALE
ALBEN RD.
THORP CL.
YORK
FOREST
TERRACE
B3018
BINFIELD ROAD
The Grange
Binfield Manor
71
Grange Cottages
Long Copse
2
BRACKNELL
BLUE MOUNTAIN GOLF CENTRE
Golf Driving Range
Park Fm.
Club House
HADDENHURST CT.
OAKMEDE PL.
EMMETS NEST
EMMETS
HILLSIDE
PITTS CL.
CHENEY CL.
Binfield C of E Prim. Sch.
CRESSEX CL.
AVON CT.
ANGEL PL.
Binfield Hall (Newbold Sch.)
WAY
BLAMIRE DR.
WILSTRODE AV.
BOLTONS
Tinkers Copse
HARVEST RIDE
Frampton's Bri.
Manor Farm
MATTHEWS CHASE
Jock's Copse
Rec Grd.
Ten. Cts.
3
FOREST
ROEBUCK EST.
CHAPEL LA.
CHAPEL TER.
Pope's Wood
WOODIES CL.
Newbold School
Moor Close
RG42
MURRELL HILL
ST. MARK'S ROAD
POPESWOOD
DUNFORD PL.
MUNDAY CT.
BLOUNT CRES
DELLER ST.
CROCKFD. PL.
LANE
COPPICE GRN.
WEYCROFTS
ENGLEMERE
COPPICE GN.
HALLBROOKE
ASPEY CT.
WEBB CL.
CULVERCROFT
GREEN
JOCK'S ROAD
MOORDALE
PRIESTWOOD
Meadow Vale Primary Sch.
EASTBURY
QUEENSWAY
AVENUE
6
170
PRIESTWOOD
Popes Meadow
Parkham
Popeswood Lodge
ROAD
LAWRENCE GRO.
NEVELLE CL.
SAMPSON PK.
WOKINGHAM RD.
WILWOOD
CAMPION HO.
BRYONY HO.
BROADLANDS
WARREN DOWN
HAWKSWOOD HO.
KINGS MERE
FARM CL.
PLOUGHLUS
SALTIRE GDS.
Comm. Cen.
PRIESTWOOD CT. RD.
WINDLESHAM
WINDMILL RD.
4
Boat Ho.
Popes Manor
Hall
HOMBROOK HO.
Rounds Hill
B3408
WOKINGHAM
ROUNDS HILL
FARLEY COPSE
HOMBROOK DR.
SIMMONDS CL.
POLLARDROW
COLDBOROUGH RISE
LINDENHILL
FANES
SPENCER RD.
STONEY
HONEYHILL
Bracknell
Popes Cottage
MUTTON HILL
GOLDEN ORB WOOD
FLETCHER
TIPPITS MEAD
STATHAM CT.
Sub.
ROAD
WATERSIDE PARK INDUSTRIAL ESTATE
MILBANKE CT.
SPRINGFIELD RD.
MUTTON OAKS
JACOB CL.
BEEHIVE LA.
ARKWRIGHT DR.
CHALLIS PL.
Farleymoor Lake
MILBANKE WAY
EASTHAMPSTEAD
Dairy
MILWARD GDNS.
POCKET CL.
FM. WD.
COVES FIELD
Farley Wood
Tennis Courts
CAIN ROAD
AMEN CORNER BUSINESS PK.
SWEETWELL RD.
THE WESTERN CENTRE
BERKSHIRE CT.
5
BRACKNELL ENTERPRISE CENTRE
PHOENIX BUSINESS PARK
Farley Wood Centre
JOHN NIKE WAY
Hotel
Ski Slope
Leisure Complex
RG12
WATERSIDE PARK INDUSTRIAL ESTATE
COOKHAM RD.
DOWNMILL
DOWNMILL RD.
KILN LA.
Western Industrial Area
LONGSHOT INDUSTRIAL ESTATE
LONGSHOT
Refuse Tip
69
NORTH VIEW
A329
Sub.
WAY
Rose Farm
Amen Corner
SOUTH VIEW
Cycle Track
OLDBURY
ROAD
Gate
Wildridings
Manor Farm
Subs.
6
LANE
Riggs Copse
MOOR
BERKSHIRE
Amen Corner Crossing
Wykery Copse
Southern Industrial Area
Buckhurst Moors
Peacock Farm
LONGSHOT LANE
DONCASTLE ROAD
Factory
WILLOUGHBY
A3095
MILL
HUBBERT
GREENHOW
FOUNTAINS GTH.
WILDRIDINGS
PEACOCK LANE
BURNTHOUSE
13
4.85
ELLESFIELD AV.
Subways
Cycle Track
ENNERDALE
DEEPDALE
86
WILDR

The Hooks
Home Farm
Scotlands Fm.
Bott Bri.
Scotlands House
Darrah Farm
Nursery
NEWELL GREEN
Meml. Grd.
FOREST ROAD
B3034
CABBAGE HILL
A3095
FOREST RD.
WARFIELD
Newell Hall
Brownlow Hall
West End
Sumanga Farm
Warfield Priory
Westend Farm
WEST END LANE
WATERSPLASH LANE
Fairclough Farm
Park Farm
Ford
Long Copse
HARVEST RIDE
(PROPOSED)
NEWELL GRN.
BRACKNELL
Kennel Lane Sch.
Play Fld.
Green Acres
Recreation Ground
Frampton's Bri.
Manor Farm
BINFIELD ROAD
RG42
Rec. Grd.
Playing Field
Works
B3018
PRIESTWOOD
Meadow Vale Primary Sch.
Comm. Cen.
Inf. & Junior Schs.
Garth Hill Comprehensive School
Recreation Ground
A329
WOKINGHAM ROAD
B3408
RING
ARLINGTON SQUARE
Health Cen.
Court
Cncl. Offs.
Met. Office
RG12
PARK ROAD
B3022
LONDON ROAD
Western Ind. Area
Dairy
SKIMPED HILL
The Point Leisure Centre
THE PEEL CENTRE
Skimped Hill
Bracknell Coll.
Ckt. Grd.
Ftbl. Grd.
Prim. Sch.
Cemetery
Eastern Ind. Area
BERKSHIRE WAY
BAGSHOT RD.
CHURCH RD.
Bracknell
DOWNSHIRE WAY
A322
Playing Field
Ranelagh Comp. Sch.
THE RIDGEWAY
Tennis Cts.
Brookham House
BRACKNELL
WILDRIDINGS
MILL LANE
Adastron House
Hill
Fox Covert
14
5
86
87
71
70
69
A
B
C
D
1
2
3
4
5
6

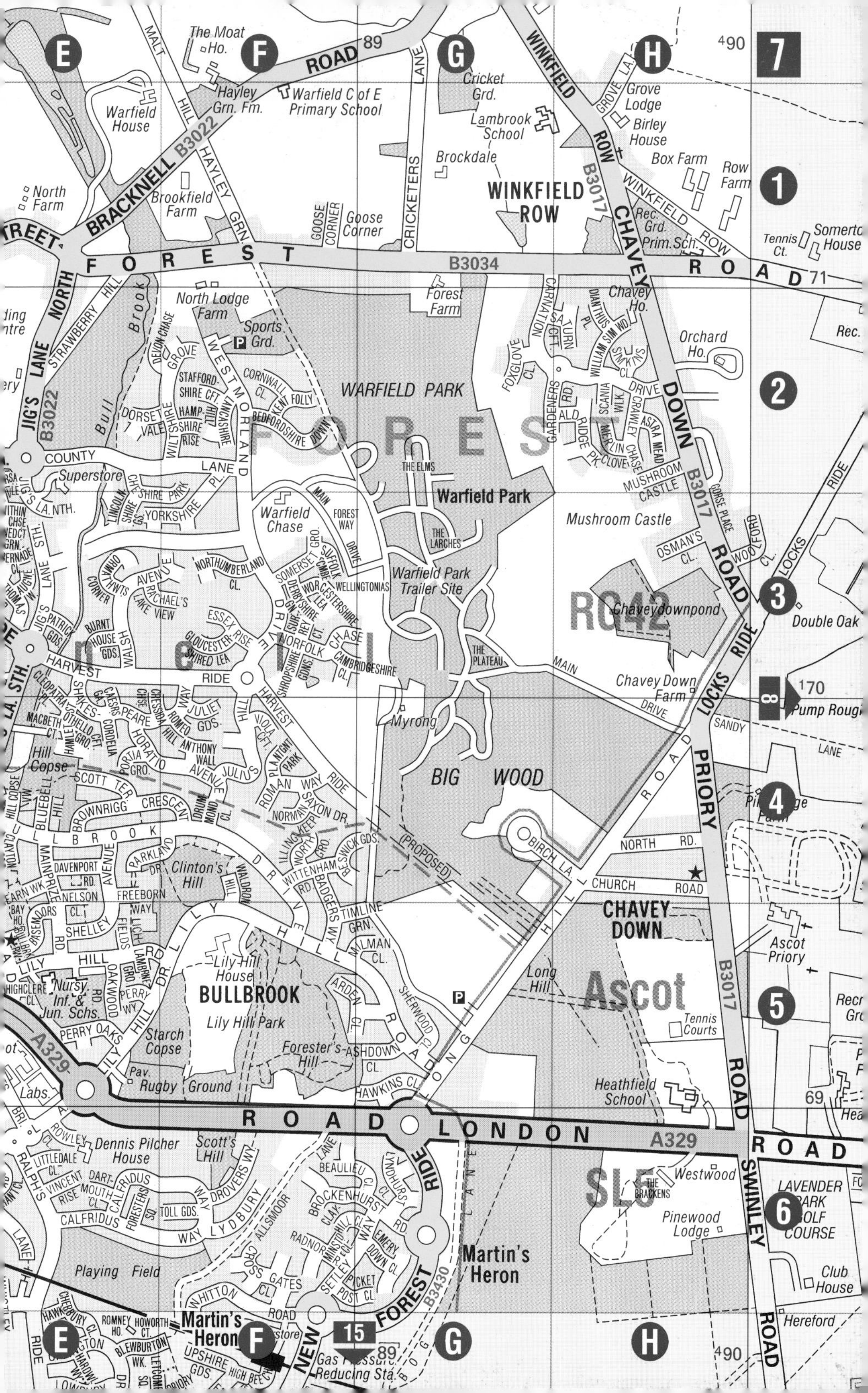

E
F
G
H
7
490
89
The Moat Ho.
Hayley Grn. Fm.
Warfield C of E Primary School
Cricket Grd.
Lambrook School
Grove Lodge
Birley House
Box Farm
Row Farm
Warfield House
North Farm
Brookfield Farm
Brockdale
Goose Corner
WINKFIELD ROW
BRACKNELL ROAD B3022
HAYLEY GRN.
MALT HILL
CRICKETERS LANE
WINKFIELD ROW B3017
CHAVEY DOWN
GROVE LA.
Rec. Grd. Prim.Sch.
Tennis Ct.
Somerton House
FOREST ROAD B3034
71
North Lodge Farm
Forest Farm
Sports Grd.
Chavey Ho.
Orchard Ho.
Rec.
WARFIELD PARK
FOREST
Warfield Park
Mushroom Castle
Warfield Chase
Warfield Park Trailer Site
RG42
Chaveydownpond
Double Oak
Chavey Down Farm
170
Pump Rough
8
BIG WOOD
CHAVEY DOWN
Ascot
Ascot Priory
Long Hill
Tennis Courts
Heathfield School
BULLBROOK
Lily Hill House
Lily Hill Park
Starch Copse
Forester's Hill
Rugby Ground
Clinton's Hill
Hill Copse
LONDON ROAD A329
A329
Dennis Pilcher House
Scott's Hill
SL5
Westwood
Pinewood Lodge
LAVENDER PARK GOLF COURSE
Club House
Hereford
Playing Field
Martin's Heron
15
Gas Pressure Reducing Sta.
1
2
3
4
5
6
69

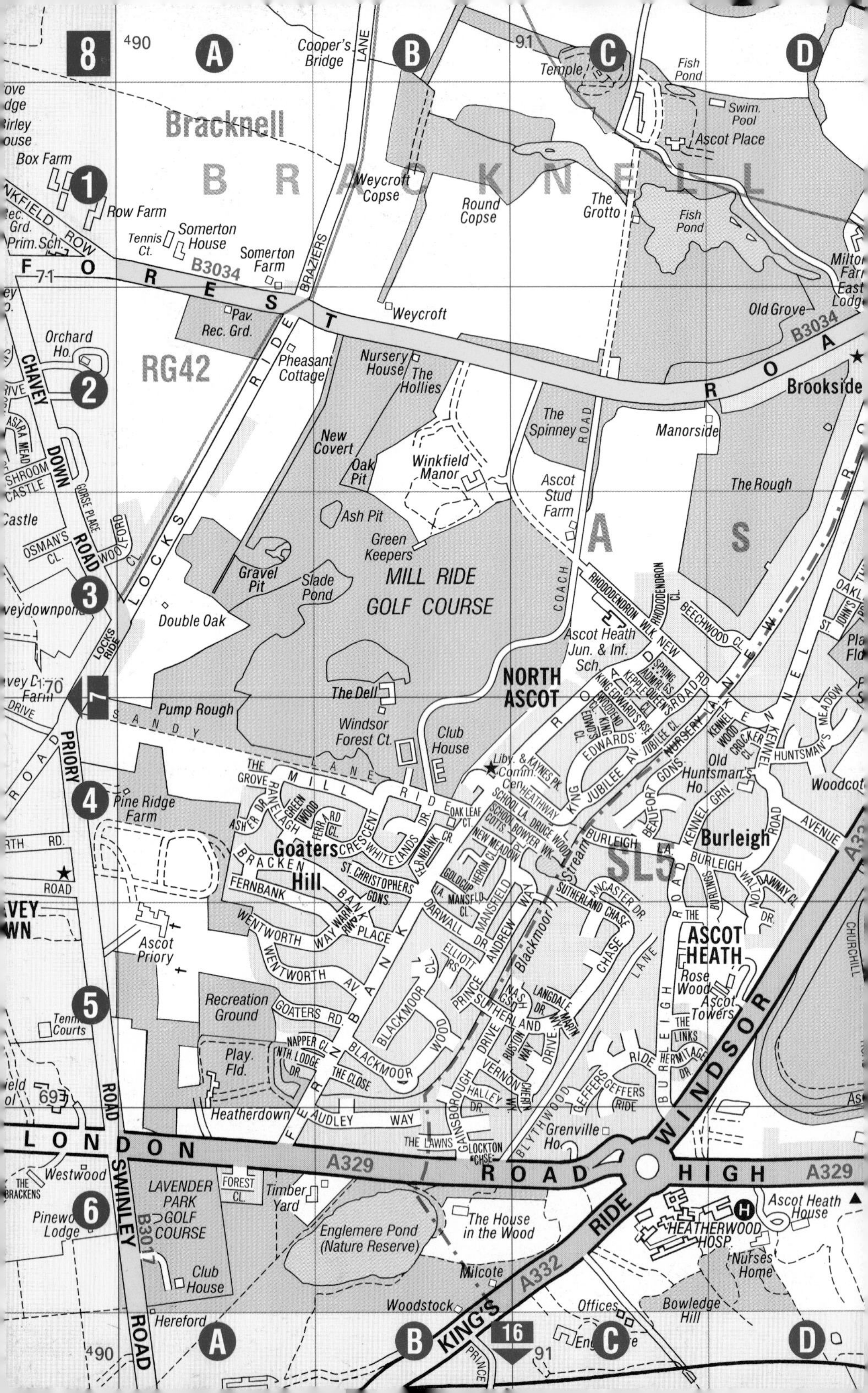
490
A
B
C
D
91
Cooper's Bridge
LANE
Temple
Fish Pond
Swim. Pool
Ascot Place
Bracknell
B R A C K N E L L
Box Farm
Row Farm
Weycroft Copse
Round Copse
The Grotto
Fish Pond
Tennis Ct.
Somerton House
Somerton Farm
Rec. Grd.
Prim. Sch.
B3034
BRAZIERS
71
F O R E S T
Pav. Rec. Grd.
Weycroft
Old Grove
B3034
Orchard Ho.
RG42
Pheasant Cottage
Nursery House
The Hollies
R O A
Brookside
CHAVEY DOWN ROAD
ASTRA MEAD
New Covert
Oak Pit
Winkfield Manor
The Spinney
ROAD
Manorside
The Rough
GORSE PLACE
WOOLFORD CL.
OSMAN'S CL.
LOCKS RIDE
Ash Pit
Green Keepers
Ascot Stud Farm
A
S
Gravel Pit
Slade Pond
MILL RIDE GOLF COURSE
COACH
RHODODENDRON WLK.
RHODODENDRON CL.
BEECHWOOD CL.
Double Oak
Ascot Heath Jun. & Inf. Sch.
NEW ROAD
NORTH ASCOT
The Dell
70
7
Pump Rough
SANDY
Windsor Forest Ct.
Club House
SPRING ADMIRALS
KEPPLE CT.
QUEEN'S RD.
KING EDWARD'S RISE
WOODEND CL.
KING EDWARDS' CL.
JUBILEE AV.
JUBILEE CL.
NURSERY LA.
KENNEL WOOD
CROCKER CL.
KENNEL LANE
HUNTSMAN'S MEADOW
BEAUFORT GDNS.
Old Huntsman's Ho.
Woodcote
PRIORY
THE GROVE
MILL RIDE
LANE
Liby. & Comm. Cen.
KAYNES PK.
HEATHWAY
SCHOOL LA.
DRUCE WOOD
SCHOOL COTTS.
BOWYER WK.
Pine Ridge Farm
ASHER DR.
RANELAGH
GREEN WOOD
FERRARD CL.
CRESCENT
WHITELANDS
OAK LEAF CT.
FERNBANK CR.
NEW MEADOW
HERON CL.
Stream
BURLEIGH LA.
KENNEL GRN.
Burleigh
AVENUE
RD.
ROAD
Goaters Hill
BRACKEN BANK
FERNBANK
ST. CHRISTOPHERS GDNS.
GOLDCUP LA.
MANSFIELD CL.
SL5
BURLEIGH
BURLINGS
WALTON DR.
DAWNAY CL.
WENTWORTH WAY
WARREN RISE
PLACE
DARWALL DR.
ANDREW WAY
Blackmoor
SUTHERLAND CHASE
LANCASTER DR.
THE ASCOT HEATH
Ascot Priory
WENTWORTH AV.
BLACKMOOR CL.
ELLIOTT RS.
PRINCE
NASH GDS.
LANGDALE DR.
MARLIN WAY
CHASE
LANE
Rose Wood
Ascot Towers
CHURCHILL
Recreation Ground
GOATERS RD.
SUTHERLAND DRIVE
RUSTON WAY
DRIVE
THE LINKS
HERMITAGE DR.
RIDE
Tennis Courts
NAPPER CL.
NTH. LODGE DR.
BLACKMOOR WOOD
VERNON
CHERN WK.
Play. Fld.
THE CLOSE
GAINSBOROUGH
HALLEY DR.
BLYTHWOOD
GEFFERS
GEFFERS RIDE
BURLEIGH
WINDSOR
69
Heatherdown
AUDLEY WAY
THE LAWNS
LOCKTON CHSE.
Grenville Ho.
L O N D O N
ROAD
A329
R O A D
H I G H
A329
Westwood
THE BRACKENS
SWINLEY
LAVENDER PARK GOLF COURSE
FOREST CL.
Timber Yard
The House in the Wood
Ascot Heath House
HEATHERWOOD HOSP.
Nurses Home
Pinewood Lodge
B3017
Club House
Englemere Pond (Nature Reserve)
Milcote
A332
RIDE
Woodstock
KING'S
Offices
Bowledge Hill
Hereford
ROAD
16
PRINCE
91
1
2
3
4
5
6

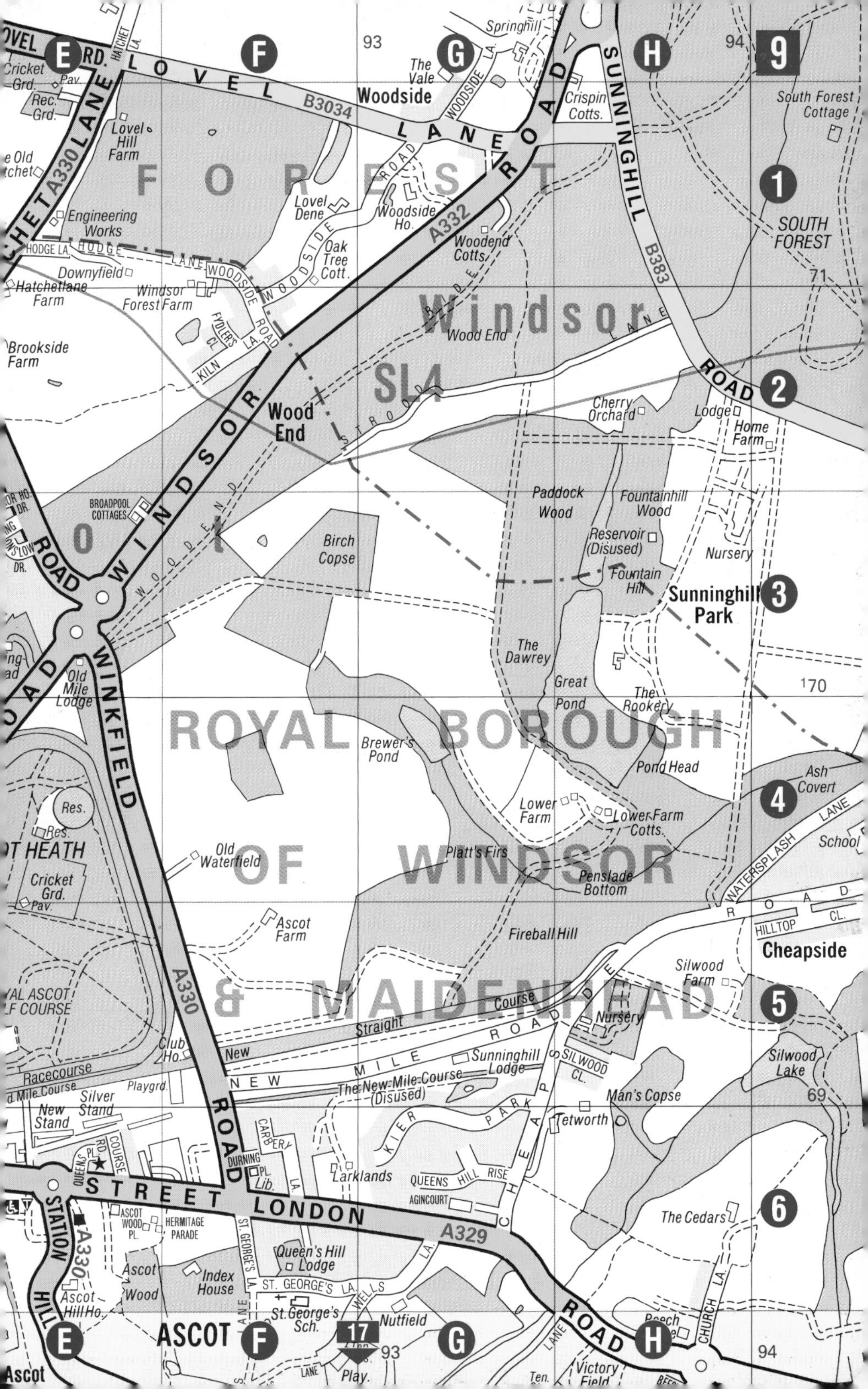
E
F
G
H
93
94
Springhill
The Vale
Woodside
LOVEL LANE
B3034
LOVEL RD.
HATCHET LA.
Cricket Grd.
Pav.
Rec. Grd.
Lovel Hill Farm
HATCHET LANE
A330
Crispin Cotts.
SUNNINGHILL
South Forest Cottage
FOREST
Lovel Dene
Woodside Ho.
WOODSIDE ROAD
A332
Engineering Works
HODGE LA.
Downyfield
Hatchetlane Farm
Windsor Forest Farm
Oak Tree Cott.
Woodend Cotts.
B383
SOUTH FOREST
71
Windsor
Wood End
FYDLERS CL.
KILN LA.
Brookside Farm
SL4
Wood End
WINDSOR ROAD
STROOD LANE
ROAD
Cherry Orchard
Lodge
Home Farm
BROADPOOL COTTAGES
Paddock Wood
Fountainhill Wood
Reservoir (Disused)
Nursery
Birch Copse
Fountain Hill
Sunninghill Park
WOODEND RIDE
Old Mile Lodge
WINKFIELD
The Dawrey
Great Pond
The Rookery
170
ROYAL BOROUGH
Brewer's Pond
Pond Head
Ash Covert
Res.
Lower Farm
Lower Farm Cotts.
School
Old Waterfield
OF WINDSOR
Platt's Firs
Penslade Bottom
WATERSPLASH LANE
HEATH
Cricket Grd.
Pav.
ROAD
HILLTOP CL.
Ascot Farm
Fireball Hill
Cheapside
Silwood Farm
ROYAL ASCOT GOLF COURSE
A330
& MAIDENHEAD
Course
Straight
Nursery
NEW MILE ROAD
Club Ho.
New
Sunninghill Lodge
SILWOOD CL.
Silwood Lake
Racecourse
Mile Course
Silver Stand
Playgrd.
The New Mile Course (Disused)
Man's Copse
69
New Stand
KIER PARK
Tetworth
CARBERY LA.
QUEENS RD.
COURSE RD.
DURNING PL.
Lib.
Larklands
QUEENS HILL RISE
CHEAPSIDE
STREET
LONDON
A329
AGINCOURT
The Cedars
STATION HILL
A330
ASCOT WOOD PL.
HERMITAGE PARADE
ST. GEORGE'S LA.
Queen's Hill Lodge
Ascot Wood
Index House
ST. GEORGE'S LA.
WELLS LA.
Ascot Hill Ho.
St. George's Sch.
Nutfield
ROAD
Beech
CHURCH LA.
ASCOT
17
93
94
Play.
Victory Field
Ascot

17

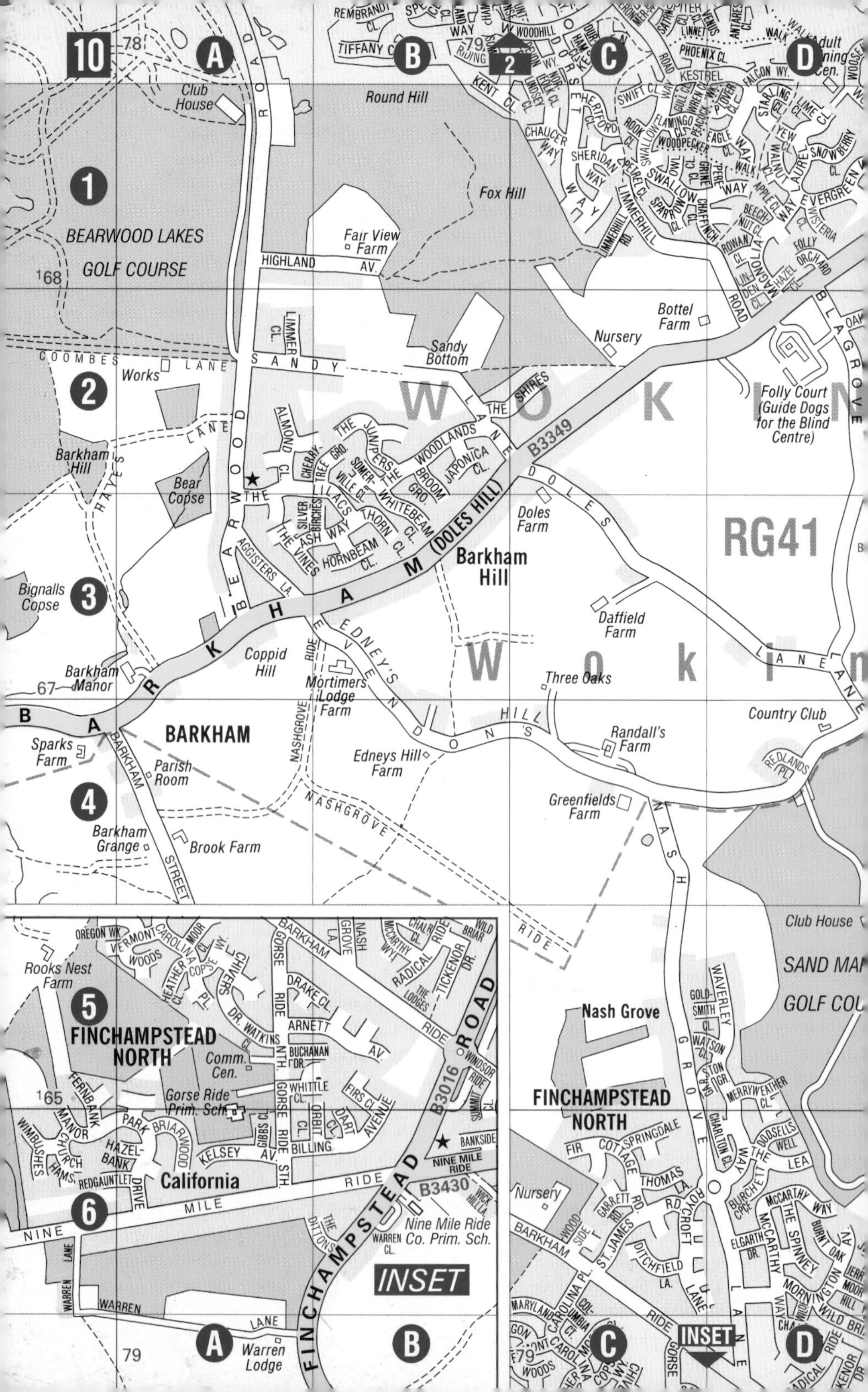

10
A
B
C
D
1
2
3
4
5
6
BEARWOOD LAKES
GOLF COURSE
Club House
Round Hill
Fox Hill
Fair View Farm
HIGHLAND AV.
Sandy Bottom
COOMBES LANE
SANDY LANE
Works
Barkham Hill
Bear Copse
Bignalls Copse
Barkham Manor
BEARWOOD ROAD
B3349
BARKHAM (DOLES HILL)
Barkham Hill
Doles Farm
DOLES LANE
Daffield Farm
Three Oaks
Coppid Hill
Mortimers Lodge Farm
EDNEY'S HILL
Edneys Hill Farm
Randall's Farm
Greenfields Farm
Country Club
REDLANDS PL.
Bottel Farm
Nursery
Folly Court
(Guide Dogs
for the Blind
Centre)
WOKINGHAM
RG41
BARKHAM
Sparks Farm
Parish Room
Barkham Grange
Brook Farm
BARKHAM STREET
NASHGROVE RIDE
NASH GROVE LANE
Club House
SAND MARTINS
GOLF COURSE
Nash Grove
FINCHAMPSTEAD
NORTH
Rooks Nest Farm
FINCHAMPSTEAD
NORTH
Comm. Cen.
Gorse Ride Prim. Sch.
California
NINE MILE RIDE
B3016
B3430
FINCHAMPSTEAD ROAD
Nine Mile Ride Co. Prim. Sch.
INSET
WARREN LANE
Warren Lodge
Nursery
INSET
78
79
168
67
165

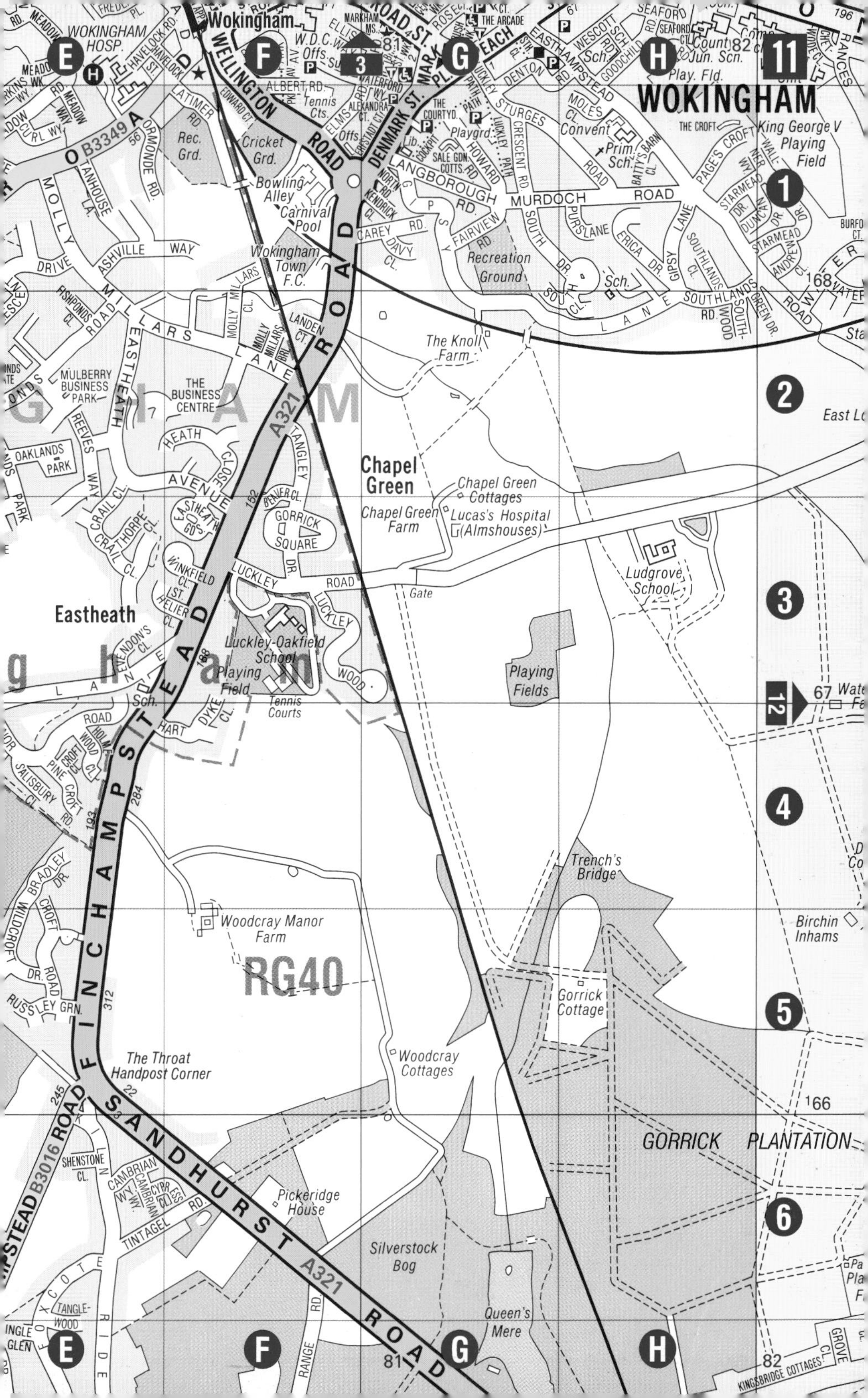

11
Wokingham
WOKINGHAM
WOKINGHAM HOSP.
WELLINGTON ROAD
DENMARK ST.
EASTHAMPSTEAD RD.
B3349
MOLLY MILLARS LANE
MILLARS ROAD
ASHVILLE WAY
TANHOUSE LA.
ORMONDE RD.
LATIMER RD.
Rec. Grd.
Cricket Grd.
Bowling Alley
Carnival Pool
Wokingham Town F.C.
CAREY RD.
DAVY CL.
LANGBOROUGH RD.
MURDOCH ROAD
FAIRVIEW RD.
Recreation Ground
SOUTH DR.
ERICA DR.
GIPSY LANE
SOUTHLANDS RD.
HOWARD RD.
CRESCENT RD.
STURGES ROAD
Convent
Prim. Sch.
King George V Playing Field
STARMEAD DR.
PAGE'S CROFT
Playgrd.
The Knoll Farm
MULBERRY BUSINESS PARK
THE BUSINESS CENTRE
EASTHEATH AVENUE
HEATH CLOSE
OAKLANDS PARK
REEVES WAY
CRAIL CL.
THORPE CL.
WINKFIELD CL.
ST. HELIER CL.
Chapel Green
Chapel Green Cottages
Chapel Green Farm
Lucas's Hospital (Almshouses)
TANGLEY DR.
GORRICK SQUARE
LUCKLEY ROAD
Gate
Ludgrove School
Eastheath
Luckley-Oakfield School
Playing Field
Tennis Courts
LUCKLEY WOOD
Playing Fields
A321
FINCHAMPSTEAD ROAD
HART DYKE CL.
SALISBURY CL.
PINE CROFT RD.
BRADLEY DR.
WILDCROFT
RUSSLEY GRN.
Woodcray Manor Farm
RG40
Trench's Bridge
Birchin Inhams
Gorrick Cottage
The Throat Handpost Corner
Woodcray Cottages
SANDHURST ROAD
B3016
SHENSTONE CL.
CAMBRIAN WY.
TINTAGEL RD.
Pickeridge House
Silverstock Bog
GORRICK PLANTATION
FOXCOTE
TANGLEWOOD
INGLE GLEN
RANGE RD.
Queen's Mere
KINGSBRIDGE COTTAGES
GROVE CL.
E
F
G
H
1
2
3
4
5
6
12
196
168
166
81
82

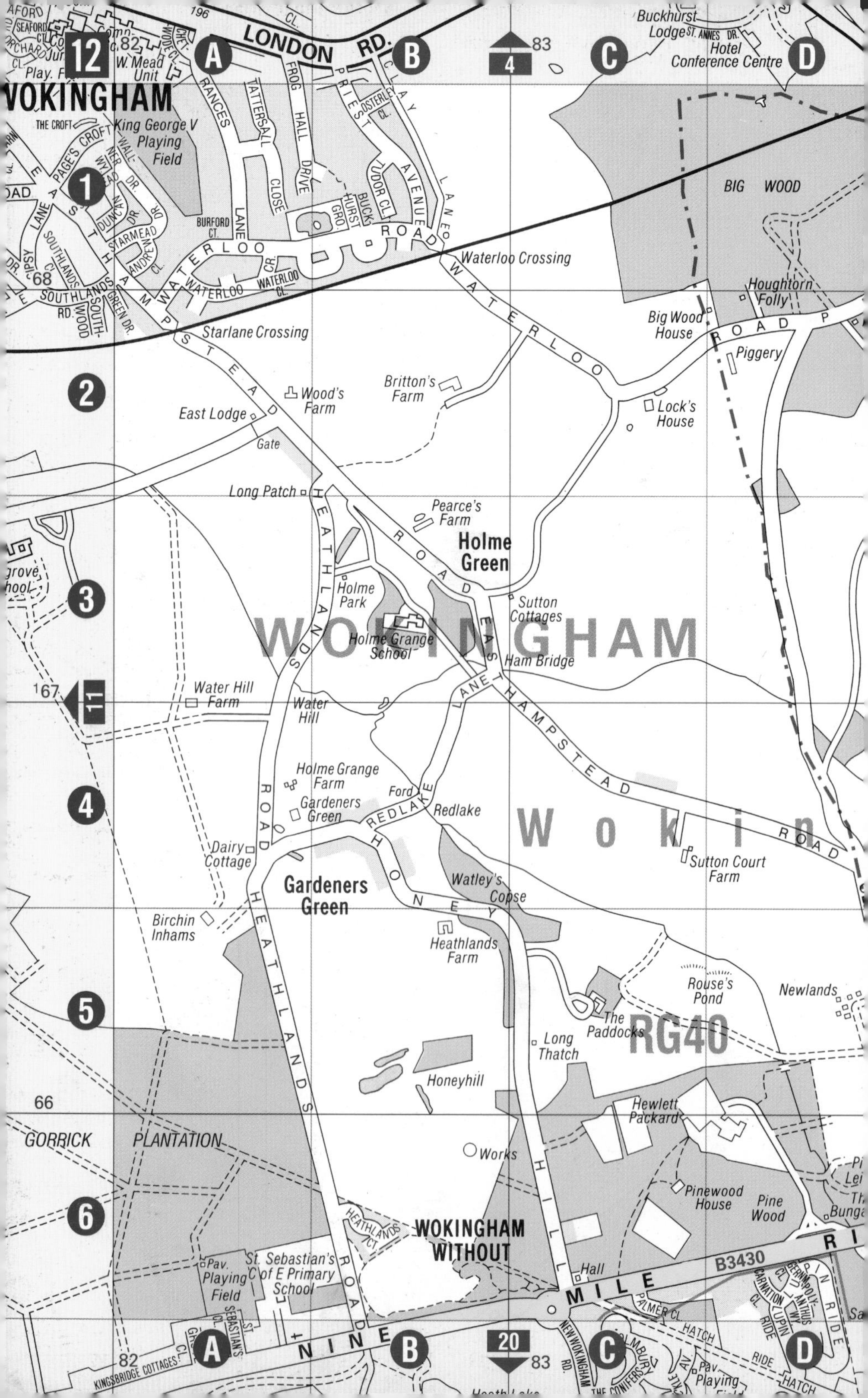
WOKINGHAM
LONDON RD.
King George V Playing Field
Waterloo Crossing
Starlane Crossing
BIG WOOD
Houghton Folly
Big Wood House
Piggery
Lock's House
Britton's Farm
Wood's Farm
East Lodge
Gate
Long Patch
Pearce's Farm
Holme Green
Sutton Cottages
Holme Park
Holme Grange School
Ham Bridge
Water Hill Farm
Water Hill
Holme Grange Farm
Ford
Gardeners Green
Redlake
Dairy Cottage
Watley's Copse
Sutton Court Farm
Birchin Inhams
Heathlands Farm
Rouse's Pond
Newlands
The Paddocks
Long Thatch
RG40
Honeyhill
Hewlett Packard
GORRICK PLANTATION
Works
Pinewood House
Pine Wood
WOKINGHAM WITHOUT
St. Sebastian's C of E Primary School
Playing Field
Hall
NINE MILE RIDE
B3430
Buckhurst Lodge
Hotel Conference Centre
WATERLOO ROAD
HEATHLANDS ROAD
HONEY HILL
EASTHAMPSTEAD ROAD
REDLAKE LANE
CLAY LANE
PRIEST AVENUE
FROG HALL DRIVE
TATTERSALL CLOSE
RANCES LANE
KINGSBRIDGE COTTAGES
NEW WOKINGHAM RD.

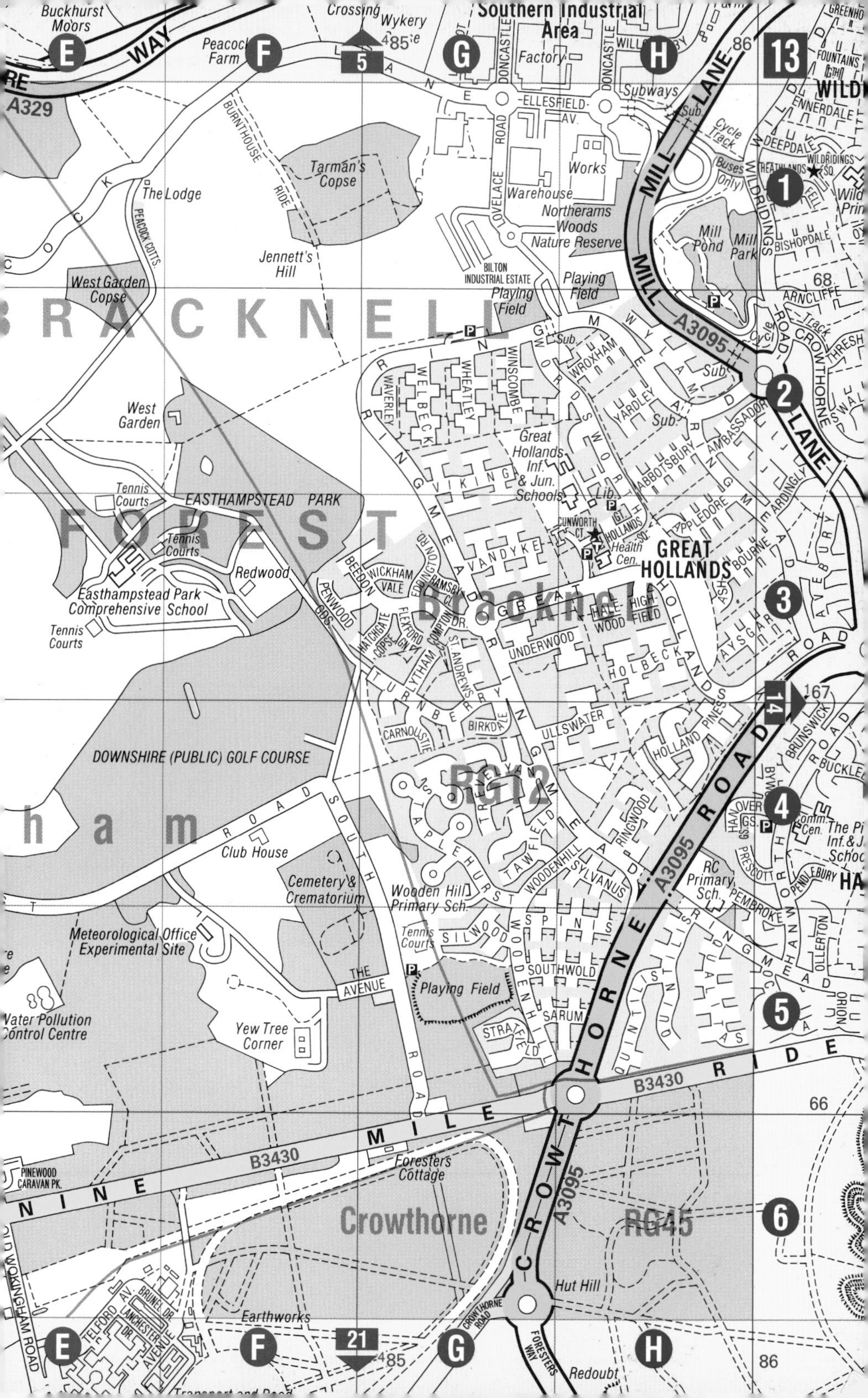

13
Buckhurst Moors
Peacock Farm
Crossing
Wykery
Southern Industrial Area
Factory
Works
Warehouse
Northerams Woods Nature Reserve
BILTON INDUSTRIAL ESTATE
Playing Field
Tarman's Copse
The Lodge
Jennett's Hill
West Garden Copse
West Garden
BRACKNELL
FOREST
EASTHAMPSTEAD PARK
Tennis Courts
Redwood
Easthampstead Park Comprehensive School
DOWNSHIRE (PUBLIC) GOLF COURSE
Club House
Cemetery & Crematorium
Meteorological Office Experimental Site
Water Pollution Control Centre
Yew Tree Corner
Wooden Hill Primary Sch.
THE AVENUE
Foresters Cottage
Crowthorne
RG45
RG12
Hut Hill
Earthworks
Redoubt
PINEWOOD CARAVAN PK.
Great Hollands Inf. & Jun. Schools
GREAT HOLLANDS
Bracknell
Health Cen.
Lib.
RC Primary Sch.
Mill Pond
Mill Park
Cycle Track
Subways
Comm. Cen.
A329
A3095
B3430
MILL LANE
CROWTHORNE ROAD
NINE MILE RIDE
RINGMEAD
WILDRIDINGS
ELLESFIELD AV.
DONCASTLE
LOVELACE ROAD
BURNTHOUSE RIDE
PEACOCK COTTS.
WAVERLEY
WELBECK
WHEATLEY
WINSCOMBE
WROXHAM
YARDLEY
AMBASSADOR
ABBOTSBURY
VIKING
VANDYKE
APPLEDORE
ARDINGLY
BOURNE
AYSGARTH
UNDERWOOD
HOLBECK
HIGH FIELD
HALEWOOD
WICKHAM VALE
PENWOOD GDS.
HATCHGATE COPSE
FLEXFORD
LYTHAM
COMPTON DR.
ST. ANDREWS
TURNBERRY
CARNOUSTIE
BIRKDALE
ULLSWATER
HOLLAND PINES
RINGWOOD
SYLVANUS
WOODENHILL
TAWFIELD
STAPLEHURST
SILWOOD
SOUTHWOLD
SARUM
STRATFIELD
QUINTILIS
HANOVER GS.
PRESCOTT
PEMBROKE
PENDLEBURY
OLLERTON
BRUNSWICK
BYWOOD
BISHOPDALE
ARNCLIFFE
DEEPDALE
ENNERDALE
HEATHLANDS SQ.
CROWTHORNE ROAD
FORESTERS WAY
OLD WOKINGHAM ROAD
TELFORD AV.
BRUNEL DR.
LANCHESTER DR.
AVENUE
E F G H
1 2 3 4 5 6
5
14
21
485
86
68
66
167

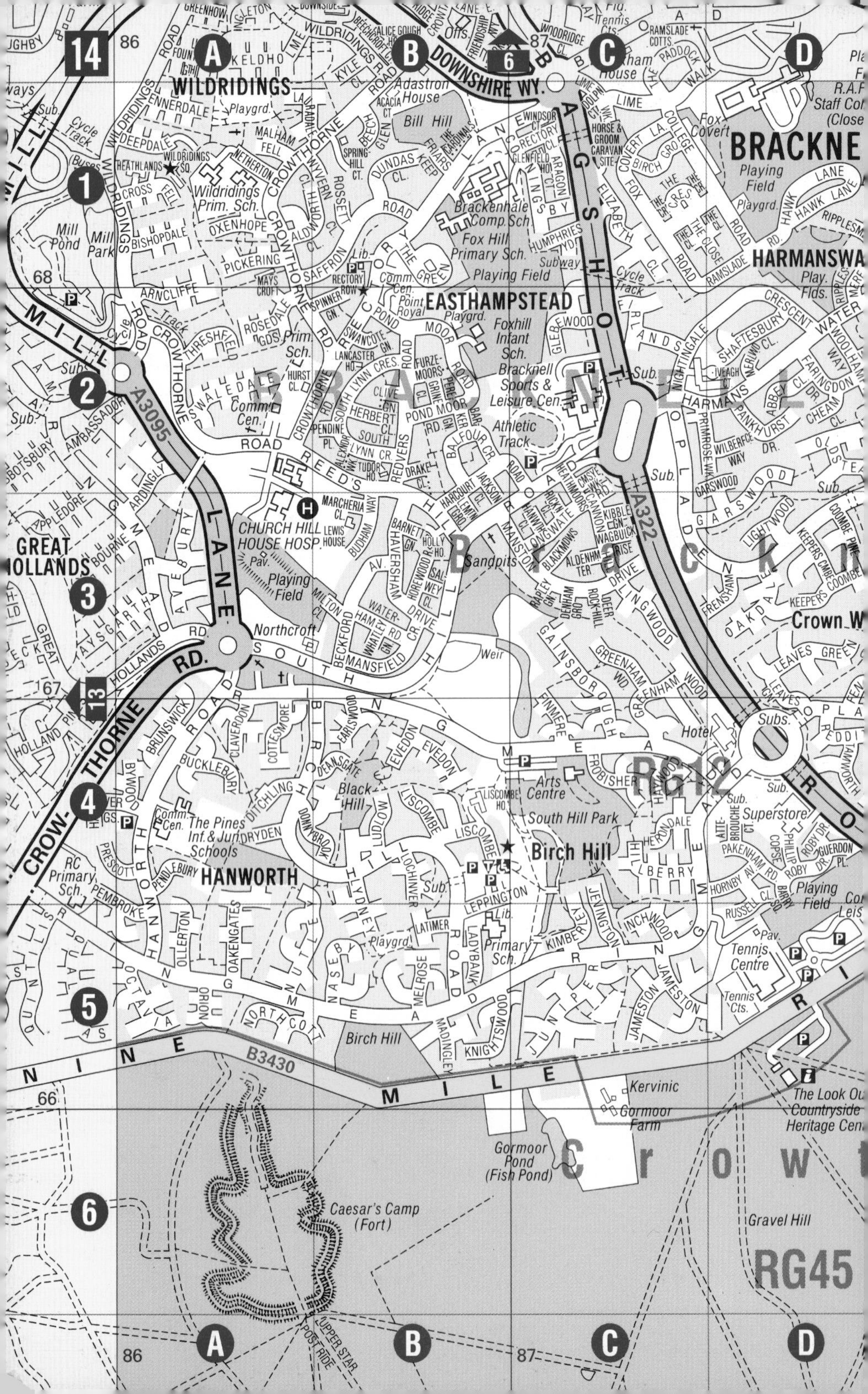
14
86
87
A
B
C
D
1
2
3
4
5
6
6
13
68
67
66
WILDRIDINGS
DOWNSHIRE WY.
Adastron House
Bill Hill
R.A.F. Staff Col. (Closed)
BRACKNELL
Playing Field
Playgrd.
HARMANSWATER
Play. Flds.
Wildridings Prim. Sch.
Mill Pond
Mill Park
Brackenhale Comp. Sch.
Fox Hill Primary Sch.
Playing Field
EASTHAMPSTEAD
Foxhill Infant Sch.
Bracknell Sports & Leisure Cen.
Athletic Track
Comm. Cen.
Prim. Sch.
A3095
A322
CROWTHORNE
ROAD
GREAT HOLLANDS
CHURCH HILL HOUSE HOSP.
Playing Field
Northcroft
Sandpits
Weir
Crown Wood
Hotel
RG12
Arts Centre
South Hill Park
Birch Hill
Black Hill
The Pines Inf. & Jun. Schools
HANWORTH
RC Primary Sch.
Superstore
Playing Field
Tennis Centre
Tennis Cts.
Primary Sch.
Birch Hill
NINE MILE RIDE
B3430
Kervinic
Gormoor Farm
Gormoor Pond (Fish Pond)
The Look Out Countryside Heritage Cen.
Caesar's Camp (Fort)
Gravel Hill
RG45
UPPER STAR POST RIDE

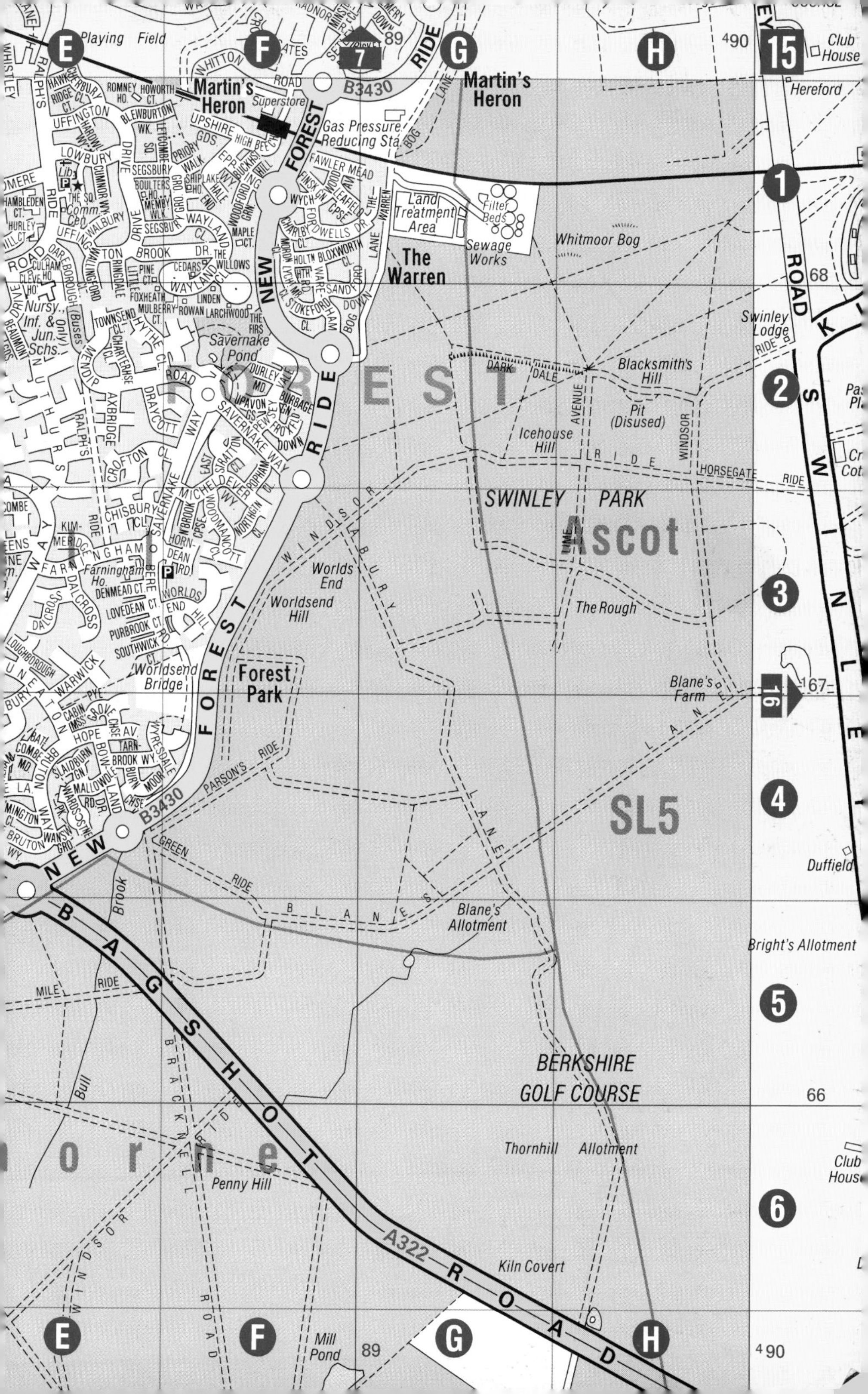

Playing Field
Martin's Heron
Superstore
Gas Pressure Reducing Sta.
Land Treatment Area
Filter Beds
Sewage Works
Whitmoor Bog
The Warren
Swinley Lodge
Blacksmith's Hill
Pit (Disused)
Icehouse Hill
FOREST
Savernake Pond
SWINLEY PARK
Ascot
Worlds End
Worldsend Hill
The Rough
Blane's Farm
Forest Park
Worldsend Bridge
Farningham Ho.
Nursy., Inf. & Jun. Schs.
SL5
Blane's Allotment
Bright's Allotment
Duffield
BERKSHIRE GOLF COURSE
Thornhill Allotment
Penny Hill
Kiln Covert
Mill Pond
Hereford
Club House
NEW FOREST RIDE
B3430
BAGSHOT ROAD
A322
WINDSOR RIDE
HORSEGATE RIDE
BLANE'S LANE
ASCOT

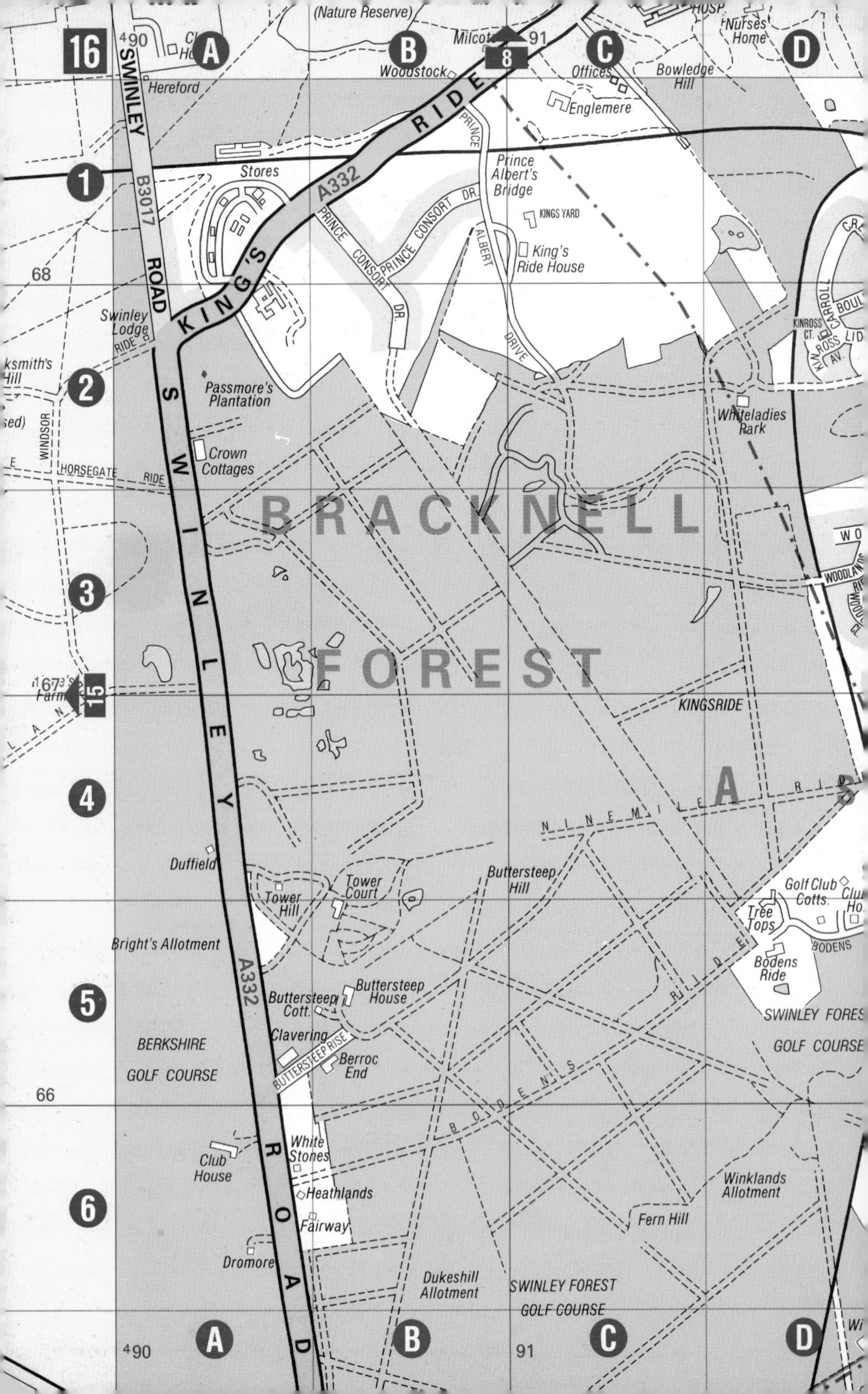

(Nature Reserve)
Milcote
8
91
HOSP.
Nurses' Home
A
B
C
D
490
Hereford
Woodstock
Offices
Bowledge Hill
Englemere
SWINLEY
KING'S RIDE
A332
PRINCE CONSORT DR.
PRINCE ALBERT DRIVE
Stores
Prince Albert's Bridge
KINGS YARD
King's Ride House
1
B3017
ROAD
68
Swinley Lodge
RIDE
2
Passmore's Plantation
WINDSOR
HORSEGATE RIDE
Crown Cottages
Whiteladies Park
KINROSS CT.
KINROSS AV.
CARROLL
BRACKNELL
FOREST
WOODLANDS
3
15
KINGSRIDE
4
NINE MILE RIDE
Duffield
Tower Hill
Tower Court
Buttersteep Hill
Golf Club Cotts.
Tree Tops
BODENS
Bodens Ride
Bright's Allotment
A332
5
Buttersteep Cott.
Buttersteep House
Clavering
BUTTERSTEEP RISE
Berroc End
BERKSHIRE GOLF COURSE
SWINLEY FOREST GOLF COURSE
66
BODENS RIDE
White Stones
Club House
Heathlands
Winklands Allotment
6
Fairway
Fern Hill
Dromore
Dukeshill Allotment
SWINLEY FOREST
GOLF COURSE
SWINLEY ROAD
A
B
C
D
490
91

17
E
F
G
H
1
2
3
4
5
6
9
18
ASCOT
Ascot
SOUTH ASCOT
SUNNINGHILL
ROYAL BOROUGH OF WINDSOR & MAIDENHEAD
SURREY HEATH
Windlesham
SL5
GU20
Queen's Hill Lodge
Index House
Ascot Wood
Ascot Hill Ho.
St. George's Sch.
Nutfield
Beech Grove
Victory Field
Playgrd.
Coombe Meadows
Marist Convent Junior Sch.
Marist Convent Senior Sch.
Swinley Prim. Sch.
Rec. Grnd.
Pinehurst
Hurstleigh
Luccombe
Maryland
St. Mary's Sch. Ascot
Errollston
Gilmuire
Playing Field
Hotel
Lowood Ho.
Forest Ridge
King's Beeches
The Kieve
West Lodge
Broadlands
Clock House
Broadlands Farm
Heathermount Sch.
Research Laboratory
Charters Sch.
Lynwood Flats
Works
Rest. (covered)
Lib.
Skears
Charlecombe
Craigmyle
Old Windsor Bog
The Belt
Keeper's Cott.
Nursery Court
Thankerton Court
New Place
Richmond Nurseries
Garden Centre
Stubbington House (School)
School Cottage
Club
Earlywood Lodge
Earlywood Orchard
Little Stream
Lavershot Hall
Lavershot Court
Windlesham Cottage
Windlemere
Lodge
Windlesham Hall
Windlesham Hall Fm.
Braids
Green Lanes
Merrywood
Warren Lodge
Little Court
Combe Edge
Devils Highway (Roman Road)
A330
A329
A30
B3020
STATION HILL
BROCKENHURST ROAD
LONDON ROAD
HIGH ST.
DEVENISH ROAD
BAGSHOT ROAD
SUNNINGHILL RD.
CORONATION ROAD
ST. MARY'S ROAD
VICTORIA ROAD
LOWER VILLAGE ROAD
UPPER VILLAGE ROAD
CHARTERS ROAD
FIREBALL HILL
BROADLANDS DRIVE
EARLEYDENE
SUNNING AV.
WESTWOOD ROAD
RAVENSDALE RD.
WHYNSTONES RD.
HURSTWOOD
FRIARY ROAD
MONKS WALK
HANCOCKS MOUNT
93
94
66
68
167

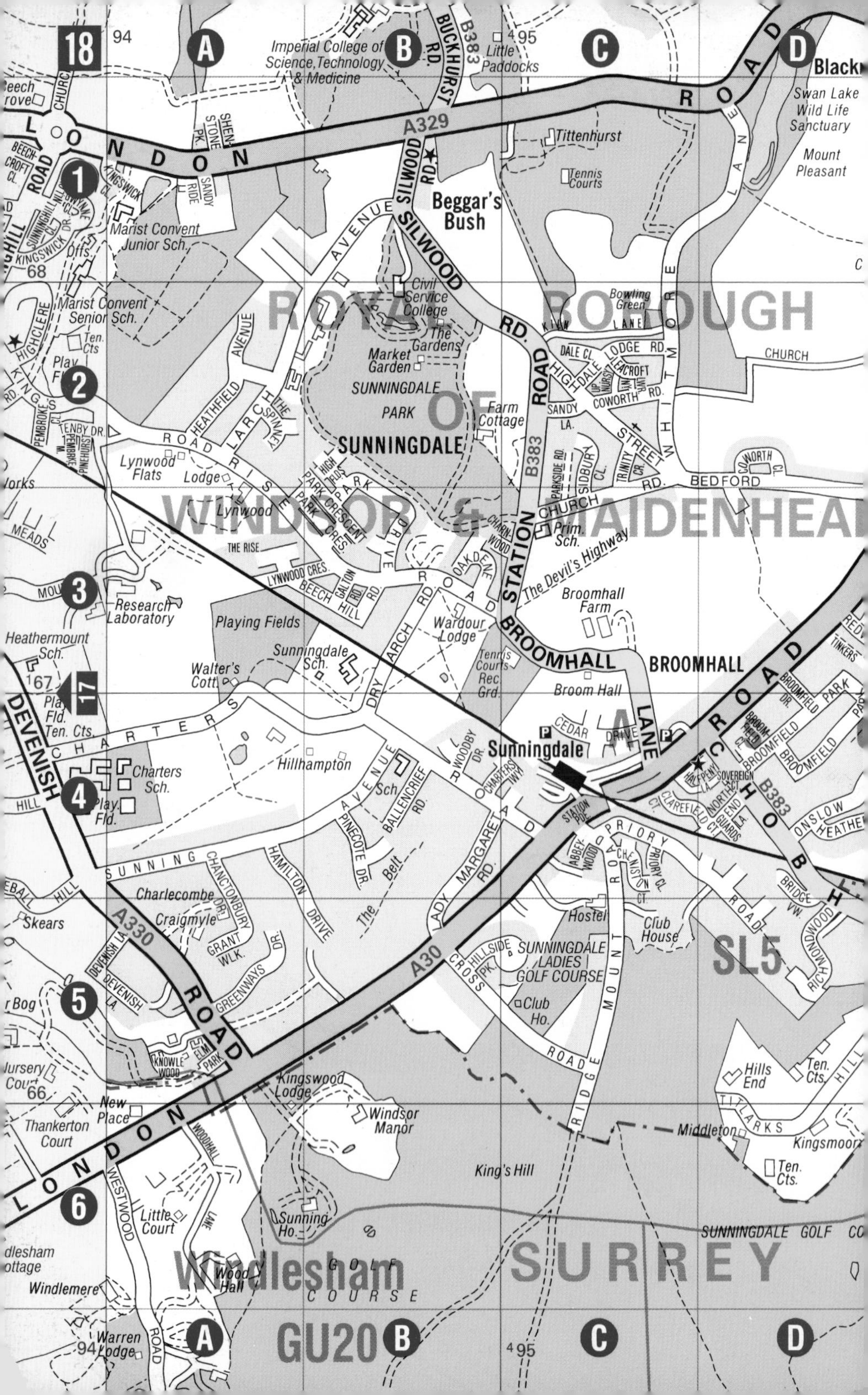

94
A
B
C
D
Imperial College of Science, Technology & Medicine
BUCKHURST RD.
B383
495
Little Paddocks
Blackn
Swan Lake Wild Life Sanctuary
Mount Pleasant
LONDON ROAD
A329
SHENSTONE PK.
SANDY RIDE
KINGSWICK CL.
SILWOOD RD.
Tittenhurst
Tennis Courts
Beggar's Bush
WHITMORE LANE
Marist Convent Junior Sch.
KINGSWICK DR.
SUNNINGHILL CL.
BEECH CROFT CL.
Offs.
68
Marist Convent Senior Sch.
AVENUE
Civil Service College
The Gardens
ROYAL BOROUGH OF WINDSOR & MAIDENHEAD
Bowling Green
KILN LANE
DALE CL.
LODGE RD.
CHURCH
HIGHCLERE
Ten. Cts.
Play. Fld.
KING'S RD.
HEATHFIELD AVENUE
LARCH AVENUE
THE SPINNEY
Market Garden
SUNNINGDALE PARK
Farm Cottage
HIGH STREET
LEACROFT
COWORTH RD.
SANDY LA.
PEMBROKE CL.
TENBY DR.
PEMBROKE M.
PINEHURST
RISE ROAD
Lynwood Flats
Lodge
SUNNINGDALE
PARKSIDE RD
SIDBURY CL.
TRINITY CR.
BEDFORD RD.
COWORTH CL.
Works
Lynwood
HIGH PARK
PARK CRESCENT
PARK DRIVE
CHURCH RD.
CHARNWOOD
Prim. Sch.
MEADS
THE RISE
LYNWOOD CRES
BEECH HILL RD.
GALTON RD.
OAKDENE
ROAD
STATION ROAD
The Devil's Highway
Broomhall Farm
3
Research Laboratory
Playing Fields
DRY ARCH RD
Wardour Lodge
BROOMHALL
Heathermount Sch.
167
17
Sunningdale Sch.
Walter's Cott.
Tennis Courts
Rec. Grd.
Broom Hall
TINKERS
DEVENISH
Play. Fld.
Ten. Cts.
CHARTERS ROAD
BROOMFIELD DR.
BROOMFIELD PARK
CEDAR DRIVE
LANE
Sunningdale
Hillhampton
WOODBY DR.
CHARTERS WAY
SOVEREIGN CT
BROOMFIELD
Charters Sch.
4
HILL
AVENUE
Sch.
BALLENCRIEF RD.
HALFPENNY LA.
NORTH END LA.
GUARDS CT.
CLAREFIELD CT.
B383
ONSLOW
HEATHER
PINECOTE DR.
STATION PDE.
ABBEYWOOD
PRIORY ROAD
CHESTON CT.
PRIORY CL.
CHOBHAM ROAD
SUNNING HILL
CHANCTONBURY DR.
HAMILTON DRIVE
LADY MARGARET RD.
The Belt
BRIDGE VW.
Charlecombe
Craigmyle
Skears
A330
GRANT WLK.
GREENWAYS DR.
Hostel
Club House
RICHMOND WOOD
SL5
DEVENISH LA.
A30
HILLSIDE PK.
CROSS ROAD
SUNNINGDALE LADIES GOLF COURSE
5
Bog
Club Ho.
RIDGE MOUNT ROAD
KNOWLE WOOD
ELM PARK
Nursery Court
66
Kingswood Lodge
Hills End
Ten. Cts.
New Place
Thankerton Court
Windsor Manor
WOODHALL
TITLARKS HILL
Middleton
Kingsmoor
King's Hill
Ten. Cts.
LONDON ROAD
6
WESTWOOD ROAD
Little Court
LANE
Sunning Ho.
Windlesham Cottage
SUNNINGDALE GOLF CO
SURREY
Windlesham
GOLF COURSE
Windlemere
Wood Hall
Warren Lodge
94
GU20
495

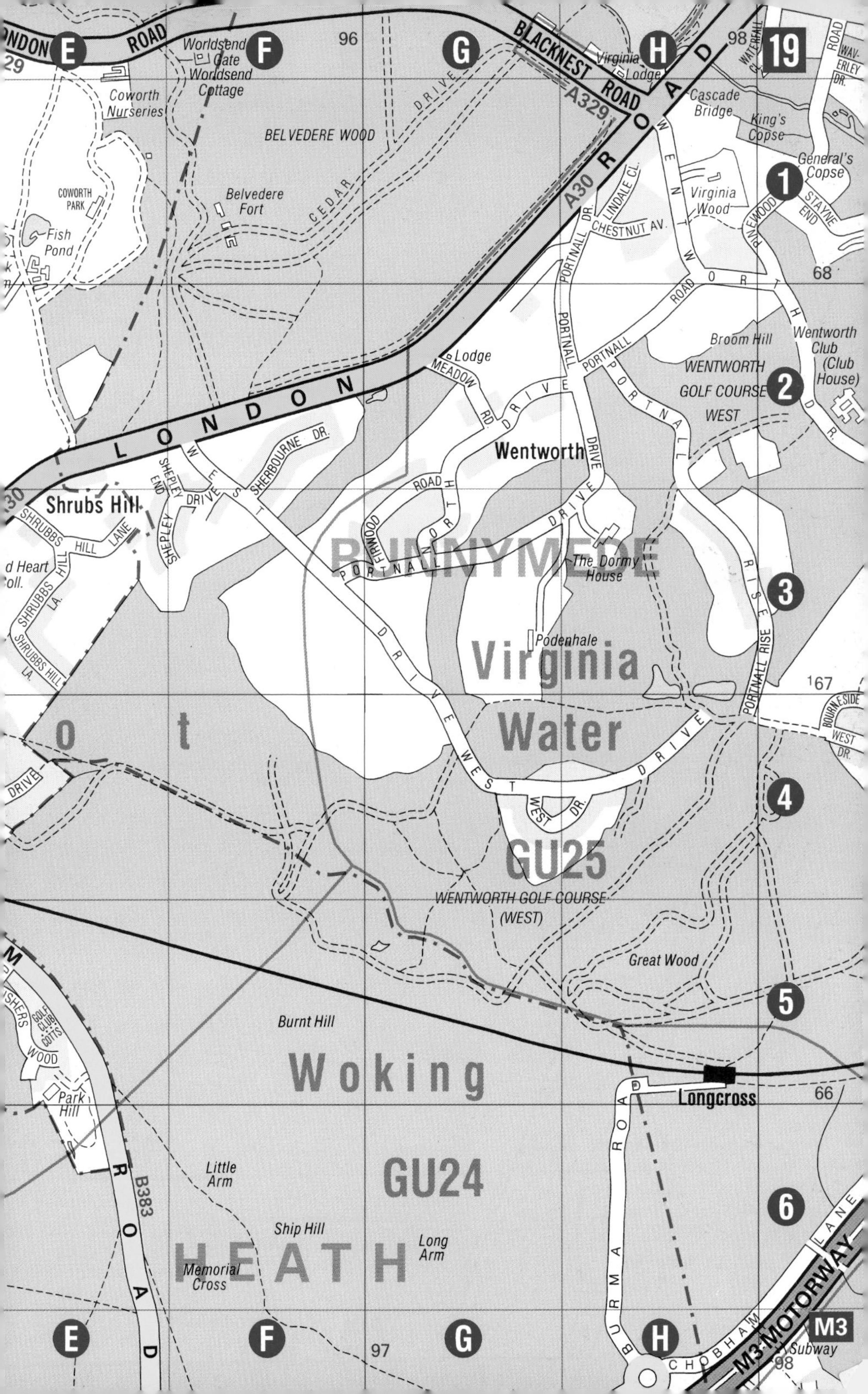
19
LONDON ROAD
Worldsend Gate
Worldsend Cottage
Coworth Nurseries
COWORTH PARK
Fish Pond
BELVEDERE WOOD
CEDAR DRIVE
Belvedere Fort
BLACKNEST ROAD
A329
A30 ROAD
Virginia Lodge
Cascade Bridge
King's Copse
General's Copse
Virginia Wood
WENTWORTH ROAD
LINDALE CL.
CHESTNUT AV.
PORTNALL DR.
PINEWOOD
STAYNE END
WAVERLEY DR.
WATERFALL CL.
Broom Hill
Wentworth Club (Club House)
WENTWORTH GOLF COURSE WEST
Lodge
MEADOW RD.
PORTNALL DRIVE
Wentworth
SHERBOURNE DR.
WEST DRIVE
SHEPLEY END
SHEPLEY DRIVE
Shrubs Hill
SHRUBBS HILL LANE
SHRUBBS HILL LA.
FIRWOOD ROAD
NORTH
PORTNALL RISE
RUNNYMEDE
The Dormy House
Podenhale
Virginia Water
BOURNESIDE
WEST DR.
GU25
WENTWORTH GOLF COURSE (WEST)
Great Wood
Burnt Hill
Woking
Longcross
GOLF CLUB COTTS
FISHERS WOOD
Park Hill
B383
Little Arm
GU24
Ship Hill
Long Arm
HEATH
Memorial Cross
BURMA ROAD
CHOBHAM LANE
M3 MOTORWAY
Subway
96
97
98
68
67
66
A30
A329

Wokingham
NINE MILE RIDE
B3430
WITHOUT
12
St. Sebastian's C of E Primary School
Heath Lake
Boat Ho.
Pineridge Farm
RG40
Ravenswood Village Settlement (Special Boarding Sch.)
The Green
WOKINGHAM
EAST BERKSHIRE GOLF COURSE
Club House
Roman Road (course of)
THE DEVIL'S HIGHWAY
LOWER WOKINGHAM RD.
A321
HOUSTON WAY
ROMAN RIDE
PRIORS WOOD
HEATH RIDE
B3348
WELLINGTONIA AV.
WELLINGTONIA ROUNDABOUT
Crowthorne
DUKE'S RIDE
WELLINGTON BUSINESS PK.
Pinewood
OAKLANDS
Oaklands Inf. & Jun. Schools
NEW WOKINGHAM ROAD
ELLIS ROAD
WATERLOO ROAD
Talbot House
Swim. Pool
Gardens Cottage
Wellington Sports Cen.
Cricket Ground
Playing Field
WELLINGTON COLLEGE
Picton House
Stanley House
Lower Lake
Upper Lake
BRACKNELL
Derby Field
Pollock Bridge
Tennis Courts
Benson House
Edgbarrowhill Star
Sandhurst Lodge
Ambarrow Hill
Ambarrow Wood
Smallbrook Bottom
Reservoir (Disused)
Edgbarrow Hill
Rosina Cottage
Sand
GU47
Coalpit Copse
Ambarrow Farm
Yonder Riding Stables
New Scotland Hill Prim. Sch.
Eagle House School
LITTLE SANDHURST
Perry Bridge Farm
CROWTHORNE ROAD
WOKINGHAM ROAD
LONGDOWN
Play. Fld.
Playing Field
22

13
Hut Hill
Earthworks
Transport and Road Research Laboratory
CROWTHORNE ROAD
B3348
FORESTERS WAY
A3095
Redoubt
Wagbullock Hill
Gorrick Well (Disused)
Windyridge
Round Hill
Hag Thorn
(ROMAN ROAD)
Devil's Highway
Butter Hill
Butter Bottom
CROWTHORNE
BROADMOOR HOSPITAL
BROADMOOR ESTATE
Cricket Grd.
Tennis Cts.
Play. Flds.
FOREST
LOWER BROADMOOR ROAD
Broadmoor Farm
Whortleberry Hill
RG45
Edgbarrow Sports Centre
Playing Field
Pine Hill
Edgbarrow Woods (Nature Reserve)
RACKSTRAW ROAD
A3095
OWLSMOOR
BROADMOOR BOTTOM
DANGER AREA
Camberley GU15
WOKINGHAM ROAD
BROOKERS ROW
CIRCLE HILL RD.
Circle Hill
NAPIER ROAD
CAMBRIDGE ROAD
BROADMOOR RD.
SOUTH MEADOW
SOUTH ROAD
OWLSMOOR ROAD
MAGDALENE ROAD
COPPER-FIELD AVENUE
23

22
A
B
C
D
20
82
83
Copse
Yonder Riding
Farm
Hill Prim. Sch.
Eagle House School
LITTLE SANDHURST
Play. Fld.
Playing Field
WOKINGHAM ROAD
HIGH STREET
LOWER SANDHURST ROAD
Perry Bridge Farm
Perry's Bridge
CHEVIOT RD.
CHILTERN RD.
AMBARROW CRESCENT
MAYBRICK CL.
ACKRELLS MEAD
CHURCH RD.
SANDY LA.
PRINCE DR.
HANCOMBE RD.
MT. PLEASANT
BARROW RISE
LONGDOWN ROAD
MICKLE HILL
LARKSWOOD CL.
SYLVAN RIDGE
OAKTREE WAY
LONG
MAXINE
PRIMROSE WAY
GREENWAYS
ACRES
BEECH
ORCHARD GATE
BROOM
Long Down
SCHOOL HILL
SCOTLAND
LAMBORNE CL.
COCK-A-DOBBY
DALE GDS.
WINDRUSH HEIGHTS
HARTS LEAP RD.
LONGDOWN LODGE
RIPPLESMORE
WELLINGTON
ST. HELENS CR.
Uplands Prim. Sch.
Hurts Hill
EAGLES NEST
MOUNTBATTEN RISE
FOREST END
WILLOW WY.
MAPLE CL.
PERRY HILL DR.
FIRTREE
ST. MICHAEL'S RD.
RECTORY CL.
MASON PL.
CEDARS CL.
McKERNAN CT.
RAY
NEW ROAD
THE NOOK
TEMPLAR CL.
Scotland Hill
MOFFATTS CL.
CROFTERS CL.
CROWTHORNE
SQUIRREL
WARREN
YORK
NEWTOWN
HONE HILL
WILLOWS END
NIGHTINGALE GDS.
SYCAMORE CL.
ALBION ROAD
RYAN MT.
ROAD
B R A C K N E L L
Sandhurst
Church Farm
Mill Farm
Mill Bridge
Blackwater River
LYCH GATE CL.
A321
YATELEY RD.
PINEWOOD CL.
CAVES FARM CL.
VALLEY VW.
STREET
YORKTOWN
Sandhurst
Works
VULCAN CL.
VULCAN WAY
GOUGH'S MDW.
Liby.
SANDHURST
Trilakes Country Park
Yateley Bridge
Depot
MILL LANE
CHANDLERS LA.
NTH. FRYERNE
W. FRYERNE
STABLE VW.
HEATHWD.
FIRGLEN DR.
WYNDHAM CL.
MILL MERE
GRN END
CHURCH VW.
THE CROFT
FRY'S LANE
CORONATION RD.
TEXTILE EST.
Yateley Industries
KEVINS DRIVE
WEYBRIDGE MEAD
SANDHURST ROAD
THE YATELEY LAKES
Sewage Works
SWAN LANE
OAKLANDS
PIPSONS
READING ROAD
PLOUGH RD.
PEMBROKE PDE.
THE PARADE
POND CROFT
Yateley Manor Prep. Sch.
Play. Flds.
STILWELL CL.
YATELEY
Sch.
LAWFORD CR.
ST. PETER'S GDNS.
HEARMON CL.
SOMERVILLE CRES.
MANOR PARK DRIVE
ROYAL OAK CL.
LODGE GRN.
PEDLARS GRO.
JENNY'S WLK.
CARRICK LA.
Yateley Inf. Sch.
CRANFORD PARK DR.
WINTON CR.
PARK
OLD
BEECHBROOK AV.
WELMORE
QUARRY
CRICKET HILL
POTLEY HILL ROAD
Yateley
CAMPBELL CL.
HATHERWOOD
ASHFIELD GREEN
B3272
ROAD
HILL CLOSE
JESSE CL.
HILFIELD
Potley Hill Prim. Sch.
PRIOR'S LA.
KELSEY GR.
COLERIDGE
CASWALL RIDE
TOLPUDDLE WY.
MASON CL.
STEVENS HILL
GORDON CR.
Darby Green
DARBY GREEN
BEECHNUT DR.
SANDHURST
Clark's Farm
Works
Pond Farm
OLDE FARM DR.
WOODVILLE CL.
DARBY GREEN ROAD
THE BIRCHES
BROOKSBY
Yateley Comm.
THE SYCAMORES
FARM
BRAMLEY LA.
LANE
THE LABURNUMS
WOODBRIDGE
CYPRESS WY.
ASPIN WY.
GLOBE
LARCHES WY.
Playing Field
Frogmore Community School
Frogmore Inf. & Ju. Schs.
H A R
WENTWORTH CL.
DENHAM DR.
HENLEY GDS.
BEAVER LANE
Cricket Hill
MANOR CR.
HALL FARM
BN FLD.
HLY ACE.
CHURCHILL CR.
MAPLE GDNS.
HANDFORD LANE
LIT. CROFT
DRIVE
MICHAELMAS CL.
WALNUT CL.
BARTONS DR.
TUDOR
CRICKET HILL
HEATHLANDS CT.
Thriftswood
GU46
COBBETT'S LANE
Hill Farm
Heathlands Cemetery
Wyndham's Pool
YATELEY COMMON COUNTRY PARK
Leafy Oak Farm
Cottage Farm
Hayward's Cottage
Picnic Area
GU17
1
2
3
4
5
6
62
160
40
79
116
2

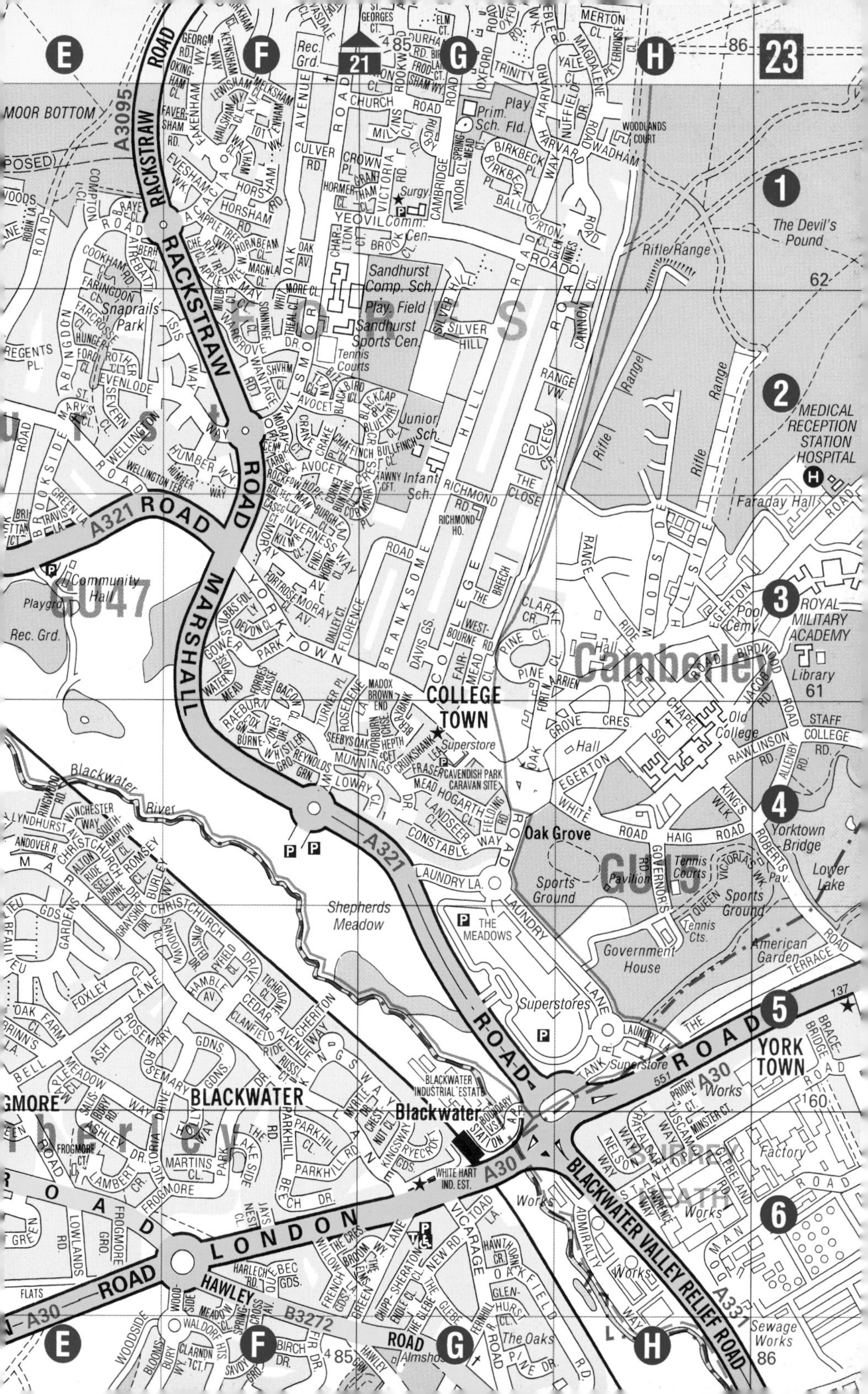

23
E
F
G
H
1
2
3
4
5
6
21
MOOR BOTTOM
RACKSTRAW ROAD
A3095
COMPTON
Snaprails Park
REGENTS PL.
ABINGDON
EVENLODE
SEVERN CL.
WELLINGTON CL.
BROOKSIDE
A321 ROAD
Community Hall
Playgrd.
GU47
Rec. Grd.
MARSHALL ROAD
YORKTOWN
Sandhurst Comp. Sch.
Play. Field
Sandhurst Sports Cen.
Tennis Courts
Junior Sch.
Infant Sch.
Surgy.
Comm. Cen.
Prim. Sch. Fld.
Play.
CULVER RD.
CROWN PL.
YEOVIL
VICTORIA RD.
CHURCH ROAD
CAMBRIDGE RD.
OXFORD RD.
MERTON CL.
TRINITY
HARVARD RD.
BIRKBECK PL.
WADHAM
WOODLANDS COURT
FOREST
SILVER HILL
RANGE VW.
COLLEGE CR.
THE CLOSE
RICHMOND RD.
RICHMOND HO.
BRANKSOME HILL
COLLEGE RD.
COLLEGE TOWN
Superstore
CAVENDISH PARK CARAVAN SITE
Rifle Range
Range
The Devil's Pound
62
MEDICAL RECEPTION STATION HOSPITAL
Faraday Hall
ROYAL MILITARY ACADEMY
Library
61
Pool
Cemy.
Camberley
Old College
STAFF COLLEGE RD.
RAWLINSON RD.
Hall
Oak Grove
WHITE ROAD
HAIG ROAD
Sports Ground
Pavilion
Tennis Courts
GU15
Yorktown Bridge
Lower Lake
Government House
American Garden
TERRACE
Blackwater River
Shepherds Meadow
THE MEADOWS
Superstores
LAUNDRY LA.
LAUNDRY LANE
A321 ROAD
BLACKWATER
Blackwater
BLACKWATER INDUSTRIAL ESTATE
STATION
WHITE HART IND. EST.
A30 ROAD
LONDON ROAD
YORK TOWN
Works
Factory
SURREY HEATH
BLACKWATER VALLEY RELIEF ROAD
A331
Sewage Works
86
60
137
551
HAWLEY
B3272
FROGMORE
FROGMORE RD.
KINGS WAY
VICARAGE ROAD
OAKFIELD ROAD
The Oaks
Almshos.
FOXLEY
ROSEMARY LANE
CHRISTCHURCH DRIVE
LYNDHURST AV.
4 85

# INDEX TO STREETS

## HOW TO USE THIS INDEX

1. Each street name is followed by its Postal District and then by its map reference; e.g. Abingdon Rd. *Sand* —2E **23** is in the Sandhurst Posttown and is to be found in square 2E on page **23.**
A strict alphabetical order is followed in which Av., Rd., St., etc. (though abbreviated) are read in full and as part of the street name; e.g. Bayley Ct. appears after Bay Ho. but before Bay Rd.

2. Streets and a selection of Subsidiary names not shown on the Maps, appear in the index in *Italics* with the thoroughfare to which it is connected shown in brackets; e.g. *Crowthorne Lodge. Brack —1B* ***14*** *(off Crowthorne Rd.)*

## GENERAL ABBREVIATIONS

All : Alley
App : Approach
Arc : Arcade
Av : Avenue
Bk : Back
Boulevd : Boulevard
Bri : Bridge
B'way : Broadway
Bldgs : Buildings
Bus : Business
Cvn : Caravan
Cen : Centre
Chu : Church
Chyd : Churchyard
Circ : Circle
Cir : Circus
Clo : Close
Comn : Common
Cotts : Cottages
Ct : Court
Cres : Crescent
Dri : Drive
E : East
Embkmt : Embankment
Est : Estate
Gdns : Gardens
Ga : Gate
Gt : Great
Grn : Green
Gro : Grove
Ho : House
Ind : Industrial
Junct : Junction
La : Lane
Lit : Little
Lwr : Lower
Mnr : Manor
Mans : Mansions
Mkt : Market
M : Mews
Mt : Mount
N : North
Pal : Palace
Pde : Parade
Pk : Park
Pas : Passage
Pl : Place
Quad : Quadrant
Rd : Road
Shop : Shopping
S : South
Sq : Square
Sta : Station
St : Street
Ter : Terrace
Trad : Trading
Up : Upper
Vs : Villas
Wlk : Walk
W : West
Yd : Yard

## POSTTOWN AND POSTAL LOCALITY ABBREVIATIONS

*Asc* : Ascot
*B'ham* : Barkham
*Binf* : Binfield
*B'water* : Blackwater
*Brack* : Bracknell
*Camb* : Camberley
*Chav D* : Chavey Down
*Chob* : Chobham
*Col T* : College Town
*Crowt* : Crowthorne
*Finch* : Finchampstead
*Frogm* : Frogmore
*Hurst* : Hurst
*N Asc* : North Ascot
*Owl* : Owlsmoor
*Sand* : Sandhurst
*Sind* : Sindlesham
*S Asc* : South Ascot
*S'dale* : Sunningdale
*S'hill* : Sunninghill
*Vir W* : Virginia Water
*Warf* : Warfield
*Warf P* : Warfield Park
*Wel C* : Wellington College
*W'sham* : Windlesham
*Wind* : Windsor
*Wink* : Winkfield
*Wink R* : Winkfield Row
*Winn* : Winnersh
*Wok* : Woking
*Wokgm* : Wokingham
*Woos* : Woosehill
*Yat* : Yateley

## INDEX TO STREETS

Christchurch Dri. *B'water* —4E **23**
Church Clo. *Winn* —2A **2**
Church Hams. *Finch* —6A **10**
Churchill Cres. *Yat* —5A **22**
Churchill Dri. *Winn* —2A **2**
Churchill Rd. *Asc* —5D **8**
Church La. *Asc* —1H **17**
(London Rd.)
Church La. *Asc* —2D **18**
(Whitmore Rd.)
Church La. *Binf* —1G **5**
Church Rd. *Asc* —1E **17**
Church Rd. *Brack* —5C **6**
Church Rd. *Chav D* —4H **7**
Church Rd. *Owl* —1G **23**
Church Rd. *Sand* —1B **22**
Church Rd. *S'dale* —3C **18**
Church Rd. E. *Crowt* —3D **20**
Church Rd. W. *Crowt* —4D **20**
Church St. *Crowt* —3D **20**
Church View. *Yat* —3A **22**
Circle Hill Rd. *Crowt* —3E **21**
Clacy Grn. *Brack* —3A **6**
Clanfield Ride. *B'water* —5F **23**
Clare Av. *Wokgm* —5G **3**
Clarefield Ct. *Asc* —4C **18**
Clarendon Clo. *Winn* —2B **2**
Clarendon Ct. *B'water* —6F **23**
Clarke Cres. *Camb* —3G **23**
Claverdon. *Brack* —4A **14**
Clayhill Clo. *Brack* —6F **7**
Clay La. *Wokgm* —6B **4**
Clayton Gro. *Brack* —4E **7**
Cleopatra Pl. *Warf* —3E **7**
Cleve Ho. *Brack* —1E **15**
Clifton Rd. *Wokgm* —4E **3**
Clintons Grn. *Brack* —4A **6**
Clive Grn. *Brack* —2B **14**
(in two parts)
Close, The. *Asc* —5B **8**
Close, The. *Brack* —1C **14**
Close, The. *Col T* —2G **23**
Clover Clo. *Wokgm* —5A **4**
Club La. *Crowt* —3F **21**
Coach Rd. *Asc* —3C **8**
Cobbett's La. *Yat* —5B **22**
Cock-A-Dobby. *Sand* —1C **22**
Cockpit Path. *Wokgm* —1G **11**
Coldborough Rise. *Brack* —4H **5**
Coleridge Av. *Yat* —5A **22**
Coleridge Clo. *Crowt* —4E **21**
College Cres. *Col T* —2G **23**
College Rd. *Brack* —1C **14**
College Rd. *Col T* —3G **23**
Columbia Cen., The. *Brack* —5B **6**
Columbia Ct. *Wokgm* —6C **10**
Comfrey Clo. *Wokgm* —4A **4**
Commons Rd. *Wokgm* —3D **2**
Compton Clo. *Brack* —3G **13**
Compton Clo. *Sand* —1E **23**
Comsaye Wlk. *Brack* —2C **14**
Coney Grange. *Warf* —2B **6**
Conifers, The. *Crowt* —1C **20**
Coningsby. *Brack* —1C **14**
Connaught Clo. *Crowt* —5B **20**
Constable Way. *Col T* —4G **23**
Cooke Rise. *Warf* —2C **6**
Cookham Clo. *Sand* —1E **23**
Cookham Rd. *Brack* —5G **5**
Coombe La. *Asc* —1G **17**
Coombe Pine. *Brack* —3D **14**
Coombes La. *Wokgm* —2A **10**
Copenhagen Wlk. *Crowt* —4D **20**
Copperfield Av. *Owl* —6G **21**
Coppice Gdns. *Crowt* —3B **20**
Coppice Grn. *Brack* —3H **5**
(in two parts)
Coppid Beech La. *Wokgm* —6C **4**
Copse Dri. *Wokgm* —5E **3**
Copse Way. *Wokgm* —5A **10**
Cordelia Croft. *Warf* —4E **7**
Corey Ho. *Brack* —5B **6**
Corfield Grn. *Wokgm* —4D **2**
Cormorant Pl. *Col T* —3G **23**
Cornbunting Clo. *Col T* —3F **23**
Corn Croft. *Warf* —3D **6**
Cornflower Clo. *Wokgm* —5B **2**
Cornwall Clo. *Warf* —2F **7**
Cornwall Clo. *Wokgm* —6B **2**
Coronation Rd. *Asc* —4E **17**
Coronation Rd. *Yat* —3A **22**
Coronation Sq. *Wokgm* —5H **3**
Corsham Way. *Crowt* —3D **20**
Cotswold Rd. *Sand* —1B **22**
Cotterell Clo. *Brack* —3B **6**
Cottesmore. *Brack* —4A **14**
County La. *Warf* —2D **6**
Course Rd. *Asc* —6E **9**
Courtyard, The. *Wokgm* —1G **11**
Covert La. *Brack* —1C **14**
Covert, The. *Asc* —4F **17**
Coves Farm Wood. *Brack* —5F **5**
Coworth Clo. *Asc* —2D **18**
Coworth Pk. *S'hill* —1E **19**
Coworth Rd. *Asc* —2C **18**
Cox Grn. *Col T* —4F **23**
Crail Clo. *Wokgm* —3E **11**
Crake Pl. *Col T* —2F **23**
Crane Ct. *Col T* —2F **23**
Cranford Pk. Dri. *Yat* —4A **22**
Crawley Chase. *Wink R* —2H **7**
Crecy Clo. *Wokgm* —6C **2**
Crescent Rd. *Wokgm* —1G **11**
Crescent, The. *B'water* —6F **23**
Crescent, The. *Brack* —1C **14**
Cressex Clo. *Binf* —2E **5**
Cressida Chase. *Warf* —4E **7**
Cricketers La. *Warf* —1G **7**
Cricket Field Gro. *Crowt* —4F **21**
Cricket Hill La. *Yat* —6A **22**
Crisp Gdns. *Binf* —3G **5**
Crocker Clo. *Asc* —4D **8**
Crockford Pl. *Binf* —3H **5**
Crocus Way. *Wokgm* —5B **2**
Croft Clo. *Wokgm* —4E **11**
Crofters Clo. *Sand* —2C **22**
Crofton Clo. *Brack* —2E **15**
Croft Rd. *Wokgm* —5E **11**
Croft, The. *Brack* —3B **6**
Croft, The. *Wokgm* —1H **11**
Croft, The. *Yat* —3A **22**
Cromwell Rd. *Asc* —1F **17**
Cross Fell. *Brack* —1A **14**
Cross Gates Clo. *Brack* —6F **7**
Cross Rd. *Asc* —5B **18**
Cross St. *Wokgm* —6G **3**
Crossway. *Brack* —5C **6**
Crown Pl. *Owl* —1G **23**
Crown Row. *Brack* —3D **14**
*Crowthorne Lodge. Brack —1B 14*
*(off Crowthorne Rd.)*
Crowthorne Rd. *Brack* —2A **14**
Crowthorne Rd. *Crowt & Brack* —2F **21**
Crowthorne Rd. *Sand* —2C **22**
Crowthorne Rd. N. *Brack* —6B **6**
Cruikshank Lea. *Col T* —4G **23**
Crutchley Rd. *Wokgm* —5H **3**
Culham Ho. *Brack* —1E **15**
Culloden Way. *Wokgm* —6C **2**
Culvercroft. *Binf* —3G **5**
Culver Rd. *Owl* —1F **23**
Cumberland Dri. *Brack* —4D **6**
Cumberland Way. *Wokgm* —6B **2**
Cumnor Way. *Brack* —1E **15**
Cunworth Ct. *Brack* —3H **13**
Curl Way. *Wokgm* —1E **11**
Cypress Clo. *Finch* —6E **11**
Cypress Way. *B'water* —5D **22**

**D**alcross. *Brack* —3E **15**
Dale Clo. *Asc* —2C **18**
Dale Gdns. *Sand* —2C **22**
Dale Lodge Rd. *Asc* —2C **18**
Dalley Ct. *Sand* —3F **23**
Danywern Dri. *Winn* —2A **2**
Darby Grn. La. *B'water* —5D **22**
Darby Grn. Rd. *B'water* —5C **22**
Darby Vale. *Warf* —2B **6**
Dark Dale. *Asc* —2G **15**
Darleydale Clo. *Owl* —6F **21**
Dart Clo. *Finch* —6B **10**
Dartmouth Clo. *Brack* —6E **7**
Darwall Dri. *Asc* —5B **8**
Dashwood Clo. *Brack* —4D **6**
Davenport Rd. *Brack* —4E **7**
Daventry Ct. *Brack* —4B **6**
Davis Gdns. *Col T* —3G **23**
Davis St. *Hurst* —1A **2**
Davis Way. *Hurst* —1B **2**
Davy Clo. *Wokgm* —1G **11**
Dawnay Clo. *Asc* —4D **8**
Deacon Clo. *Wokgm* —4G **3**
Dean Gro. *Wokgm* —5G **3**
Deansgate. *Brack* —4B **14**
Deepdale. *Brack* —1A **14**
Deepfield Rd. *Brack* —5D **6**
Deerhurst Av. *Winn* —2A **2**
Deer Rock Hill. *Brack* —3C **14**
Defford Clo. *Wokgm* —3D **2**
Delane Dri. *Winn* —3A **2**
Deller St. *Binf* —3H **5**
Dene Clo. *Brack* —3C **6**
Denham Dri. *Yat* —5A **22**
Denham Gro. *Brack* —3C **14**
Denmark St. *Wokgm* —1G **11**
Denmead Ct. *Brack* —3E **15**
Denton Rd. *Wokgm* —6G **3**
Derbyshire Grn. *Warf* —3F **7**
Derwent Clo. *Wokgm* —6C **2**
Devenish Clo. *S'hill* —3H **17**
Devenish La. *Asc* —5H **17**
Devenish Rd. *Asc* —3G **17**
Devil's Highway, The. *Crowt* —3A **20**
De Vitre Grn. *Wokgm* —5B **4**
Devon Chase. *Warf* —2E **7**
Devon Clo. *Col T* —3F **23**
Devon Clo. *Wokgm* —6C **2**
Diamond Way. *Wokgm* —5C **2**
Dianthus Pl. *Wink R* —2H **7**
Dickens Ct. *Wokgm* —6F **3**
Dieppe Clo. *Wokgm* —6C **2**
Ditchfield La. *Wokgm* —6C **10**
Ditchling. *Brack* —4A **14**
Dittons, The. *Finch* —6B **10**
Dodsells Well. *Wokgm* —6D **10**
Doles Hill. *B'ham* —3B **10**
Doles La. *Wokgm* —2C **10**
Dolphin Clo. *Winn* —3A **2**
Dolphin Ct. *Brack* —1C **14**
Doman Rd. *Camb* —6H **23**
Doncastle Rd. *Brack* —6G **5**
Donnington Pl. *Winn* —2B **2**
Donnybrook. *Brack* —4A **14**
Dormer Clo. *Crowt* —3C **20**
Dorset Vale. *Warf* —2E **7**
Dorset Way. *Wokgm* —6C **2**
Dovedale Clo. *Owl* —6F **21**
Dowding Ct. *Crowt* —2E **21**
Downmill Rd. *Brack* —5H **5**
Downshire Way. *Brack* —5A **6**
(in two parts)
Downside. *Brack* —6B **6**
Drake Clo. *Brack* —2B **14**
Drake Clo. *Wokgm* —5A **10**
Draycott. *Brack* —2E **15**
Drayton Clo. *Brack* —5D **6**
Droitwich Clo. *Brack* —6D **6**
Drovers Way. *Brack* —6F **7**
Druce Wood. *Asc* —4C **8**
Drummond Clo. *Brack* —4F **7**
Dry Arch Rd. *Asc* —3B **18**
Dryden. *Brack* —4A **14**
Dukeshill Rd. *Brack* —4B **6**
Duke's Ride. *Crowt* —4A **20**
Dukes Wood. *Crowt* —3D **20**
(in two parts)
Duncan Dri. *Wokgm* —1H **11**
Dundas Clo. *Brack* —1B **14**
Dunford Pl. *Binf* —3G **5**
Dunkirk Clo. *Wokgm* —6C **2**
Dunt La. *Hurst* —1C **2**
Durham Clo. *Wokgm* —6C **2**
Durham Rd. *Owl* —6G **21**
Durley Mead. *Brack* —2F **15**
Durning Pl. *Asc* —6F **9**
Dyer Rd. *Wokgm* —5A **4**

**E**agle Clo. *Crowt* —1C **20**
Eagle Clo. *Wokgm* —1D **10**
Eaglehurst Cotts. *Binf* —1E **5**
Eagles Nest. *Sand* —1C **22**
Earle Croft. *Warf* —3C **6**
Earleydene. *Asc* —5F **17**
Earlswood. *Brack* —4B **14**
Eastbury Ct. *Brack* —3H **5**
Eastbury Pk. *Winn* —2B **2**
Eastern La. *Crowt* —4H **21**
Eastern Rd. *Brack* —5D **6**
East Grn. *B'water* —6E **23**
Easthampstead Rd. *Brack* —5A **6**
Easthampstead Rd. *Wokgm* —6H **3**
Eastheath Av. *Wokgm* —2F **11**
Eastheath Gdns. *Wokgm* —3F **11**
E. Stratton Clo. *Brack* —2F **15**
Eddington Rd. *Brack* —3G **13**
Eden Way. *Winn* —3A **2**
Edgbarrow Ct. *Crowt* —5C **20**
Edgbarrow Rise. *Sand* —6C **20**
Edgcumbe Pk. Dri. *Crowt* —3C **20**
Edgedale Clo. *Crowt* —4D **20**
Edgewood Clo. *Crowt* —1C **20**
Edmonds Ct. *Brack* —4C **6**
Edward Ct. *Wokgm* —1F **11**
Egerton Rd. *Col T* —4H **23**
Elgar Av. *Crowt* —1D **20**
Elgarth Dri. *Finch* —6D **10**
Elizabeth Clo. *Brack* —1C **14**
Elizabeth Ct. *Wokgm* —6F **3**
Elizabeth Gdns. *Asc* —2F **17**
Elizabeth Rd. *Wokgm* —6H **3**
Ellenborough Clo. *Brack* —4D **6**
Ellesfield Av. *Brack* —1G **13**
Elliott Rise. *Asc* —5B **8**
Ellison Way. *Wokgm* —6F **3**
Ellis Rd. *Crowt* —2C **20**
Elm Ct. *Sand* —6G **21**
Elmley Clo. *Wokgm* —3D **2**
Elm Pk. *S'dale* —5A **18**
Elms Rd. *Wokgm* —1F **11**
Elms, The. *B'water* —6F **23**
Elms, The. *Warf P* —2G **7**
Emerald Clo. *Wokgm* —5C **2**
Emerson Ct. *Crowt* —3D **20**
Emery Down Clo. *Brack* —6G **7**
Emmbrook Ga. *Wokgm* —4D **2**
Emmbrook Rd. *Wokgm* —4D **2**
Emmbrook Vale. *Wokgm* —3D **2**
Emm Clo. *Wokgm* —4D **2**
Emmets Nest. *Binf* —2E **5**
Emmets Pk. *Binf* —2E **5**
Emmview Clo. *Wokgm* —5D **2**
Enborne Gdns. *Brack* —3D **6**
Englemere Rd. *Brack* —3H **5**
Ennerdale. *Brack* —1A **14**
Epping Way. *Brack* —1F **15**
Erfstadt Ct. *Wokgm* —1G **11**
Erica Dri. *Wokgm* —1H **11**
Essame Clo. *Wokgm* —6H **3**
Essex Rise. *Warf* —3F **7**
Eustace Cres. *Wokgm* —4H **3**
Evedon. *Brack* —4B **14**
Evendon's Clo. *Wokgm* —3E **11**
Evendon's La. *Wokgm* —3B **10**
Evenlode Way. *Sand* —2E **23**
Everest Rd. *Crowt* —2D **20**
Evergreen Way. *Wokgm* —1D **10**
Evesham Wlk. *Owl* —1F **23**
Exchange Rd. *Asc* —2G **17**

**F**aircross. *Brack* —6B **6**
Fairfax. *Brack* —4A **6**

High St. Crowthorne. *Crowt* —4E **21**
High St. Little Sandhurst. *Sand* —1B **22**
High St. Sandhurst. *Sand* —1B **22**
High St. Sunningdale. *S'dale* —2C **18**
High St. Sunninghill. *S'hill* —2H **17**
Highway. *Crowt* —3C **20**
Hilfield. *Yat* —5B **22**
Hillary Dri. *Crowt* —2D **20**
Hillberry. *Brack* —4C **14**
Hill Copse View. *Brack* —4E **7**
Hilliary Dri. *Crowt* —2D **20**
Hillside. *Asc* —2G **17**
Hillside. *Camb* —3H **23**
Hillside Dri. *Binf* —2E **5**
Hillside Pk. *S'dale* —5B **18**
Hilltop Clo. *Asc* —5H **9**
Hinton Clo. *Crowt* —1D **20**
Hinton Dri. *Crowt* —1D **20**
Hitherhooks Hill. *Binf* —4G **5**
Hodge La. *Wink* —1E **9**
(in two parts)
Hogarth Clo. *Col T* —4G **23**
Holbeck. *Brack* —3H **13**
Holland Pines. *Brack* —4H **13**
Holly Acre. *Yat* —5A **22**
Hollyhook Clo. *Crowt* —2C **20**
Holly Ho. *Brack* —3B **14**
Holly Spring Cotts. *Brack* —3D **6**
Holly Spring La. *Brack* —4C **6**
Holly Way. *B'water* —6F **23**
Holmbury Av. *Crowt* —1C **20**
Holme Clo. *Crowt* —1C **20**
Holmes Clo. *Asc* —3G **17**
Holmes Clo. *Wokgm* —2E **11**
Holmes Cres. *Wokgm* —2D **10**
Holmewood Clo. *Wokgm* —4E **11**
Holt La. *Wokgm* —5F **3**
Holton Heath. *Brack* —1F **15**
Hombrook Dri. *Brack* —4G **5**
Hombrook Ho. *Brack* —4G **5**
Hone Hill. *Sand* —2D **22**
Honey Hill. *Wokgm* —4B **12**
Honeyhill Rd. *Brack* —4A **6**
Honeysuckle Clo. *Crowt* —1C **20**
Hope Av. *Brack* —4E **15**
Hope Cotts. *Brack* —6C **6**
Hopeman Clo. *Col T* —3F **23**
Horatio Av. *Warf* —4E **7**
Horewood Rd. *Brack* —3B **14**
Hormer Clo. *Owl* —1F **23**
Hornbeam Clo. *Owl* —1F **23**
Hornbeam Clo. *Wokgm* —3B **10**
Hornby Av. *Brack* —4D **14**
Horndean Rd. *Brack* —3F **15**
Horsegate Ride. *Asc* —3E **17**
(Coronation Rd.)
Horsegate Ride. *Asc* —2H **15**
(Swinley Rd.)
Horse & Groom Cvn. Site. *Brack* —1C **14**
Horsham Rd. *Owl* —1F **23**
Horsnape Gdns. *Binf* —2D **4**
Horsneile La. *Brack* —3B **6**
Houston Way. *Crowt* —3A **20**
Howard Rd. *Wokgm* —1G **11**
Howell Clo. *Warf* —2C **6**
Howorth Ct. *Brack* —1E **15**
Hubberholme. *Brack* —6A **6**
Hughes Rd. *Wokgm* —5H **3**
Humber Clo. *Wokgm* —5C **2**
Humber Way. *Sand* —2F **23**
Humphries Yd. *Brack* —1C **14**
Hungerford Clo. *Sand* —2E **23**
Huntingdonshire Clo. *Wokgm* —6B **2**
Huntsgreen Ct. *Brack* —5C **6**
Huntsmans Meadow. *Asc* —4D **8**
Hurley Ct. *Brack* —1E **15**
Hurst Clo. *Brack* —2A **14**
Hurstwood. *Asc* —3E **17**
Huson Rd. *Warf* —2C **6**
Hutsons Clo. *Wokgm* —4H **3**
Hythe Clo. *Brack* —2E **15**

Illingworth Gro. *Brack* —4F **7**
Inchwood. *Brack* —5C **14**
Ingle Glen. *Finch* —6E **11**
Ingleton. *Brack* —6A **6**
Innings La. *Warf* —4E **7**
Inverness Way. *Col T* —3F **23**
Isis Clo. *Winn* —3A **2**
Isis Way. *Sand* —2F **23**
Iveagh Ct. *Brack* —2D **14**

Jackson Clo. *Brack* —2B **14**
Jacob Clo. *Brack* —5F **5**
Jacob Rd. *Col T* —3H **23**
Jameston. *Brack* —5C **14**
Japonica Clo. *Wokgm* —2B **10**
Jasmine Clo. *Wokgm* —5B **2**
Jays Nest Clo. *B'water* —6F **23**
Jennys Wlk. *Yat* —4A **22**
Jerrymoor Hill. *Finch* —6D **10**
Jesse Clo. *Yat* —5B **22**
Jevington. *Brack* —5C **14**
Jig's La. *Warf* —4E **7**
Jig's La. N. *Warf* —2E **7**
Jig's La. S. *Warf* —4E **7**
Jock's La. *Brack* —4G **5**
John Nike Way. *Brack* —5E **5**
Joseph Ct. *Warf* —2E **7**
Jubilee Av. *Asc* —4C **8**
Jubilee Av. *Wokgm* —5E **3**
Jubilee Clo. *Asc* —4C **8**
Jubilee Ct. *Brack* —6C **6**
Juliet Gdns. *Warf* —4F **7**
Julius Hill. *Warf* —4F **7**
Juniper. *Brack* —5C **14**
Junipers, The. *Wokgm* —2B **10**
Jupiter Way. *Wokgm* —6C **2**
Jutland Clo. *Wokgm* —6C **2**

Kaynes Pk. *Asc* —4C **8**
Keates Grn. *Brack* —4B **6**
Keats Way. *Crowt* —1D **20**
Keble Way. *Owl* —6G **21**
Keepers Coombe. *Brack* —3D **14**
Keephatch Rd. *Wokgm* —4A **4**
Kelburne Clo. *Winn* —1A **2**
Keldholme. *Brack* —6A **6**
Kelsall Pl. *Asc* —4E **17**
Kelsey Av. *Wokgm* —6A **10**
Kelsey Gro. *Yat* —5A **22**
Kendrick Clo. *Wokgm* —1G **11**
Kenilworth Av. *Brack* —4D **6**
Kennel Av. *Asc* —4D **8**
Kennel Clo. *Asc* —2D **8**
Kennel Grn. *Asc* —4C **8**
Kennel La. *Brack* —3B **6**
Kennel Ride. *Asc* —4D **8**
Kennel Wood. *Asc* —4D **8**
Kennet Ct. *Wokgm* —6D **2**
Kent Clo. *Wokgm* —1B **10**
Kent Folly. *Warf* —2F **7**
Kentigern Dri. *Crowt* —3F **21**
Kenton Clo. *Brack* —5D **6**
Kesteven Way. *Wokgm* —6C **2**
Kestrel Way. *Wokgm* —6C **2**
Ketcher Grn. *Binf* —1E **5**
Kevins Dri. *Yat* —3A **22**
Keynsham Way. *Owl* —6F **21**
Kibble Grn. *Brack* —3C **14**
Kier Pk. *Asc* —6G **9**
Kilmington Clo. *Brack* —4E **15**
Kilmuir Clo. *Col T* —3F **23**
Kiln La. *Asc* —2C **18**
Kiln La. *Brack* —5A **6**
Kiln La. *Wink* —2F **9**
Kiln Ride. *Finch* —6E **11**
Kimberley. *Brack* —5C **14**
Kimmeridge. *Brack* —3E **15**
King Edward's Clo. *Asc* —4C **8**
King Edward's Rise. *Asc* —3C **8**
King Edward's Rd. *Asc* —4C **8**
Kingsbridge Cotts. *Wokgm* —6H **11**
King's Keep. *Sand* —1D **22**
Kingsley Clo. *Crowt* —5D **20**
Kingsmere Rd. *Brack* —4H **5**
King's Ride. *Asc* —2A **16**
King's Rd. *Asc* —2H **17**
King's Rd. *Crowt* —4D **20**
King St. La. *Winn* —3A **2**
King's Wlk. *Col T* —4H **23**
Kingsway. *B'water* —5F **23**
Kingswick Clo. *Asc* —1H **17**
Kingswick Dri. *Asc* —1H **17**
Kings Yd. *Asc* —1C **16**
Kinross Av. *Asc* —2D **16**
Kinross Ct. *Asc* —2D **16**
Kirkham Clo. *Owl* —6F **21**
Knightswood. *Brack* —5B **14**
Knole Wood. *Asc* —5A **18**
Knowles Av. *Crowt* —3B **20**
Knox Grn. *Binf* —1E **5**
Kyle Clo. *Brack* —6B **6**

Laburnum Rd. *Winn* —3A **2**
Laburnums, The. *B'water* —5D **22**
Lackman's Hill. *Brack* —2B **6**
Ladybank. *Brack* —5B **14**
Lady Margaret Rd. *Asc* —5B **18**
Lake End Way. *Crowt* —4C **20**
Lakeside. *Brack* —3C **6**
Lakeside, The. *B'water* —6F **23**
Lalande Clo. *Wokgm* —6C **2**
Lambert Cres. *B'water* —6E **23**
Lamborne Clo. *Sand* —1C **22**
Lambourne Gro. *Brack* —5E **7**
Lammas Mead. *Binf* —3G **5**
Lancashire Hill. *Warf* —2F **7**
Lancaster Ho. *Brack* —2B **14**
Lanchester Dri. *Crowt* —1E **21**
Landen Ct. *Wokgm* —2F **11**
Landseer Clo. *Col T* —4G **23**
Langborough Rd. *Wokgm* —1G **11**
Langdale Dri. *Asc* —5C **8**
Larch Av. *Asc* —2A **18**
Larch Av. *Wokgm* —5E **3**
Larches, The. *Warf P* —3G **7**
Larches Way. *B'water* —5D **22**
Larchwood. *Brack* —2F **15**
Larges Bri. Dri. *Brack* —6C **6**
Larges La. *Brack* —5C **6**
Larkspur Clo. *Wokgm* —5B **2**
Larkswood Clo. *Sand* —1C **22**
Larkswood Dri. *Crowt* —3D **20**
Latimer. *Brack* —5B **14**
Latimer Rd. *Wokgm* —1F **11**
Laud Way. *Wokgm* —6A **4**
Laundry La. *Sand* —4G **23**
Lauradale. *Brack* —1A **14**
Laurel Clo. *Wokgm* —1D **10**
*Laurel Ct. Brack —1F 15*
*(off Wayland Clo.)*
Lawford Cres. *Yat* —4A **22**
Lawns, The. *Asc* —6B **8**
Lawrence Clo. *Wokgm* —6H **3**
Lawrence Gro. *Binf* —4F **5**
Lawrence Way. *Camb* —6H **23**
Lawson Way. *Asc* —3D **18**
Leacroft. *Asc* —2C **18**
Lea Croft. *Crowt* —2D **20**
Leafield Copse. *Brack* —1F **15**
Lea, The. *Wokgm* —6D **10**
Leaves Grn. *Brack* —3D **14**
Leicester. *Brack* —4E **15**
Leith Clo. *Crowt* —1C **20**
Lemington Gro. *Brack* —3B **14**
Leney Clo. *Wokgm* —4H **3**
Lenham Clo. *Winn* —3C **2**
Leppington. *Brack* —4B **14**
Letcombe Sq. *Brack* —1E **15**
Letcomb Sq. *Brack* —1E **15**
Leverkusen Rd. *Brack* —6B **6**
Lewisham Way. *Owl* —1F **23**
Lewis Ho. *Brack* —3B **14**
Ley Side. *Crowt* —3C **20**
Lichfields. *Brack* —5E **7**
Liddell Way. *Asc* —2D **16**
Lightwood. *Brack* —3D **14**
Lilacs, The. *Wokgm* —2B **10**
Lilley Ct. *Crowt* —4D **20**
Lily Hill Dri. *Brack* —5E **7**
Lily Hill Rd. *Brack* —5E **7**
Lime Av. *Asc* —3H **15**
Lime Clo. *Wokgm* —1D **10**
Limerick Clo. *Brack* —4A **6**
Lime Wlk. *Brack* —1C **14**
Limmer Clo. *Wokgm* —2A **10**
Limmerhill Rd. *Wokgm* —1C **10**
Lincolnshire Gdns. *Warf* —3E **7**
Lindale Clo. *Vir W* —1H **19**
Linden. *Brack* —2F **15**
Linden Clo. *Wokgm* —1D **10**
Lindenhill Rd. *Brack* —4H **5**
Lindsey Clo. *Wokgm* —1C **10**
Lingwood. *Brack* —3C **14**
Links, The. *Asc* —5C **8**
Linkway. *Crowt* —3B **20**
Linnet Wlk. *Wokgm* —6C **2**
Liscombe. *Brack* —4B **14**
Liscombe Ho. *Brack* —4B **14**
Lit. Croft. *Yat* —6A **22**
Littledale Clo. *Brack* —6E **7**
Lit. Hill Rd. *Hurst* —1B **2**
Lit. Moor. *Sand* —1E **23**
Lit. Ringdale. *Brack* —1E **15**
Llangar Gro. *Crowt* —3C **20**
Llanvair Clo. *Asc* —3E **17**
Llanvair Dri. *Asc* —3D **16**
Lochinver. *Brack* —4B **14**
Locks Ride. *Asc* —3H **7**
Lockton Chase. *Asc* —6B **8**
Lodge Gro. *Yat* —4B **22**
Lodges, The. *Finch* —5B **10**
London Rd. *Asc & S'hill* —6F **9**
London Rd. *B'water* —6D **22**
London Rd. *Brack & Asc* —5D **6**
London Rd. *Sand* —5H **23**
London Rd. *S'dale* —5B **18**
London Rd. *Vir W* —2G **19**
London Rd. *W'sham* —6G **17**
London Rd. *Wokgm & Binf* —6H **3**
Longdon Rd. *Winn* —3A **2**
Longdown Lodge. *Sand* —2D **22**
Longdown Rd. *Sand* —1C **22**
Long Hill Rd. *Asc* —5G **7**
Long La. *Wok* —2B **4**
Long Mickle. *Sand* —1C **22**
Longmoors. *Brack* —4G **5**
Longshot Ind. Est. *Brack* —5G **5**
Longshot La. *Brack* —6G **5**
(in two parts)
Long's Way. *Wokgm* —5A **4**
Longwater Rd. *Brack* —3C **14**
Loughborough. *Brack* —3E **15**
Lovedean Ct. *Brack* —3E **15**
Lovelace Rd. *Brack* —1G **13**
Lovel La. *Wink* —1F **9**
Lovel Rd. *Wink* —1E **9**
Lowbury. *Brack* —1E **15**
Lwr. Broadmoor Rd. *Crowt* —4E **21**
Lwr. Church Rd. *Sand* —1A **22**
Lwr. Moor. *Yat* —5A **22**
Lwr. Nursery. *Asc* —2C **18**
Lwr. Sandhurst Rd. *Finch & Sand* —6A **20**
Lwr. Village Rd. *Asc* —2F **17**
Lwr. Wokingham Rd. *Finch & Crowt* —2A **20**
Lowlands Rd. *B'water* —6E **23**
Lowry Clo. *Col T* —4F **23**
Lowther Clo. *Wokgm* —4D **2**
Lowther Rd. *Wokgm* —3C **2**
Luckley Path. *Wokgm* —6G **3**
Luckley Rd. *Wokgm* —3F **11**
Luckley Wood. *Wokgm* —3F **11**
Ludlow. *Brack* —4B **14**
Lupin Ride. *Crowt* —1D **20**

Page's Croft. *Wokgm* —1H **11**
Paice Grn. *Wokgm* —5H **3**
Pakenham Rd. *Brack* —4D **14**
Palmer Clo. *Wokgm* —6C **12**
Palmer Ct. *Wokgm* —6G **3**
Palmer School Rd. *Wokgm* —6G **3**
Pankhurst Dri. *Brack* —2D **14**
Parade, The. *Yat* —5A **22**
Park Av. *Wokgm* —1F **11**
(in two parts)
Park Cres. *Asc* —3B **18**
Park Dri. *Asc* —3B **18**
Parkhill Clo. *B'water* —6F **23**
Parkhill Rd. *B'water* —6F **23**
Parkland Dri. *Brack* —4E **7**
Park La. *Binf* —3G **5**
Park Rd. *Brack* —5D **6**
Park Rd. *Sand* —3E **23**
Park Rd. *Wokgm* —6F **3**
Parkside Rd. *Asc* —2C **18**
Parkway. *Crowt* —3C **20**
Parsons Field. *Sand* —2D **22**
Parson's Ride. *Brack* —4F **15**
Pathway, The. *Binf* —1E **5**
Patrick Gdns. *Warf* —3E **7**
Patten Ash Dri. *Wokgm* —5A **4**
Payley Dri. *Wokgm* —4A **4**
Peach St. *Wokgm* —6G **3**
Peacock Cotts. *Brack* —1E **13**
Peacock La. *Wokgm & Brack* —2D **12**
Peacock Wlk. *Wokgm* —1C **10**
Peddlars Gro. *Yat* —4A **22**
Peel Cen., The. *Brack* —5A **6**
Peggotty Pl. *Owl* —6G **21**
Pembroke. *Brack* —4H **13**
Pembroke Clo. *Asc* —2H **17**
Pembroke M. *Asc* —2H **17**
Pembroke Pde. *Yat* —4A **22**
Pendine Pl. *Brack* —2B **14**
Pendlebury. *Brack* —4A **14**
Pensford Clo. *Crowt* —1D **20**
Penwood Gdns. *Brack* —3F **13**
Peregrine Clo. *Brack* —2B **14**
Peregrine Clo. *Wokgm* —1D **10**
Perkins Way. *Wokgm* —1E **11**
Perryhill Dri. *Sand* —1B **22**
Perry Oaks. *Brack* —5E **7**
Perry Way. *Brack* —5E **7**
Peterhouse Clo. *Owl* —6H **21**
Petrel Clo. *Wokgm* —1C **10**
Pewsey Vale. *Brack* —2F **15**
Pheasant Clo. *Winn* —2A **2**
Phillip Copse. *Brack* —4D **14**
Phoenix Bus. Pk. *Brack* —5E **5**
Phoenix Clo. *Wokgm* —6C **2**
Pickering. *Brack* —1A **14**
Picket Post Clo. *Brack* —6F **7**
Pigott Rd. *Wokgm* —4H **3**
Pine Clo. *Sand* —3G **23**
Pinecote Dri. *Asc* —4B **18**
Pine Ct. *Brack* —1E **15**
Pine Croft Rd. *Wokgm* —4E **11**
Pine Dri. *B'water* —6G **23**
Pine Dri. *Finch* —6E **11**
Pinefields Clo. *Crowt* —3D **20**
Pinehill Rise. *Sand* —2E **23**
Pinehill Rd. *Crowt* —4D **20**
Pinehurst. *S'hill* —2H **17**
Pinewood Av. *Crowt* —2E **21**
Pinewood Cvn. Pk. *Wokgm* —6E **13**
Pinewood Clo. *Sand* —2B **22**
Pinewood Rd. *Vir W* —1H **19**
Pipsons Clo. *Yat* —4A **22**
Pitch Pl. *Binf* —1F **5**
Pitts Clo. *Binf* —2F **5**
Plantagenet Pk. *Warf* —4F **7**
Plateau, The. *Warf P* —3G **7**
Ploughlands. *Brack* —4H **5**
Plough La. *Wokgm* —5B **4**
Plough Rd. *Yat* —3A **22**
Plover Clo. *Wokgm* —1D **10**
Pocket Clo. *Binf* —5F **5**
Pollardrow Av. *Brack* —4H **5**
(in two parts)
Polyanthus Way. *Crowt* —6D **12**
Pond Croft. *Yat* —4A **22**
Pond Moor Rd. *Brack* —2B **14**
Popeswood Rd. *Binf* —3F **5**
Popham Clo. *Brack* —2F **15**
Poplar La. *Winn* —1B **2**
Poplars, The. *Asc* —2E **17**
Poppy Pl. *Wokgm* —6F **3**
Porchester. *Asc* —1E **17**
Portia Gro. *Warf* —4E **7**
Portman Clo. *Brack* —4A **6**
Portnall Dri. *Vir W* —3G **19**
Portnall Rise. *Vir W* —2H **19**
Portnall Rd. *Vir W* —2H **19**
Potley Hill Rd. *Yat* —4B **22**
Poyle Gdns. *Brack* —4D **6**
Prescott. *Brack* —4H **13**
Prides Crossing. *Asc* —3E **9**
Priest Av. *Wokgm* —1B **12**
Priestwood Av. *Brack* —4H **5**
Priestwood Ct. Rd. *Brack* —4A **6**
Priestwood Sq. *Brack* —4A **6**
Priestwood Ter. *Brack* —4A **6**
Primrose La. *Winn* —1A **2**
Primrose Wlk. *Brack* —2C **14**
Primrose Way. *Sand* —1D **22**
Prince Albert Dri. *Asc* —1B **16**
Prince Andrew Way. *Asc* —5B **8**
Prince Consort Dri. *Asc* —1B **16**
Prince Dri. *Sand* —1C **22**
Princess Sq. *Brack* —5B **6**
Prior's La. *B'water* —5C **22**
Priors Wood. *Crowt* —4A **20**
Priory Clo. *Asc* —4C **18**
Priory Ct. *Camb* —5H **23**
Priory Ct. *Winn* —1A **2**
Priory La. *Brack* —3C **6**
Priory Rd. *Chav D* —4H **7**
Priory Rd. *S'dale* —4C **18**
Priory, The. *Winn* —1A **2**
Priory Wlk. *Brack* —1F **15**
Proctors Rd. *Wokgm* —6B **4**
Purbrook Ct. *Brack* —3E **15**
Purcell Rd. *Crowt* —1D **20**
Purslane. *Wokgm* —1H **11**
Pyegrove Chase. *Brack* —4E **15**

**Q**uadrant Ct. *Brack* —6E **7**
Qualitas. *Brack* —5H **13**
Quarry La. *Yat* —5A **22**
Quartz Clo. *Wokgm* —5B **2**
Quebec Gdns. *B'water* —6F **23**
Queen's Clo. *Asc* —3C **8**
Queens Hill Rise. *Asc* —6G **9**
Queens Pine. *Brack* —3E **15**
Queens Pl. *Asc* —6E **9**
Queen's Rd. *Asc* —2H **17**
Queensway. *Brack* —4H **5**
Queen Victoria's Wlk. *Col T* —4H **23**
Quelm La. *Brack* —2B **6**
Quince Clo. *Asc* —1G **17**
Quintilis. *Brack* —5H **13**
(in two parts)

**R**achael's Lake View. *Warf* —3F **7**
Rackstraw Rd. *Sand* —1E **23**
Radcliffe Way. *Brack* —4G **5**
Radical Ride. *Finch* —5B **10**
Radnor Rd. *Brack* —6F **7**
Raeburn Way. *Col T* —4F **23**
Rainbow Pk. *Winn* —3A **2**
Ralph's Ride. *Brack* —6E **7**
(in two parts)
Ramsbury Clo. *Brack* —3G **13**
Ramslade Cotts. *Brack* —6C **6**
Ramslade Rd. *Brack* —1D **14**
Ranald Ct. *Asc* —2E **9**
Rances La. *Wokgm* —1A **12**
Randall Mead. *Binf* —2D **4**
Ranelagh Cres. *Asc* —4A **8**
Ranelagh Dri. *Brack* —6C **6**
Range Ride. *Camb* —3H **23**
Range Rd. *Finch* —6F **11**
Range View. *Col T* —2G **23**
Rapley Grn. *Brack* —3C **14**
Ravensdale Rd. *Asc* —2E **17**
Ravenswood Av. *Crowt* —3A **20**
Rawlinson Rd. *Camb* —4H **23**
Reading Rd. *Winn & Wokgm* —2A **2**
Reading Rd. *Yat* —3A **22**
Rectory Clo. *Brack* —1C **14**
Rectory Clo. *Sand* —2B **22**
Rectory Clo. *Wokgm* —6G **3**
Rectory La. *Brack* —2B **14**
Rectory Rd. *Wokgm* —6G **3**
Rectory Row. *Brack* —1B **14**
Redditch. *Brack* —4D **14**
Redgauntlet. *Finch* —6A **10**
Redlake La. *Wokgm* —4B **12**
Redlands Pl. *Wokgm* —4D **10**
Red Rose. *Binf* —1E **5**
Redvers Rd. *Brack* —2B **14**
Redwood Dri. *Asc* —3D **18**
Reed's Hill. *Brack* —2B **14**
Reeves Way. *Wokgm* —2E **11**
Regents Pl. *Sand* —2E **23**
Regents Wlk. *Asc* —4G **17**
Rembrandt Clo. *Wokgm* —6B **2**
Reynards Clo. *Winn* —2A **2**
Reynolds Grn. *Col T* —4F **23**
Rhododendron Clo. *Asc* —3C **8**
Rhododendron Wlk. *Asc* —3C **8**
Richmond Ho. *Sand* —3G **23**
Richmond Rise. *Wokgm* —5C **2**
Richmond Rd. *Col T* —2G **23**
Richmondwood. *Asc* —5D **18**
Rickman Clo. *Brack* —3C **14**
Ridge Mt. Rd. *Asc* —5C **18**
Ridgeway, The. *Brack* —6C **6**
Riding Way. *Wokgm* —6B **2**
Ringmead. *Brack* —2G **13**
Ring, The. *Brack* —5C **6**
Ringwood. *Brack* —4H **13**
Ringwood Clo. *Asc* —1F **17**
Ringwood Rd. *B'water* —4E **23**
Ripplesmere. *Brack* —1D **14**
Ripplesmore Clo. *Sand* —2D **22**
Rise Rd. *Asc* —2A **18**
Rise, The. *Crowt* —3B **20**
Rise, The. *S'dale* —3A **18**
Rise, The. *Wokgm* —5E **3**
Roberts Gro. *Wokgm* —2D **10**
Roberts Rd. *Camb* —4H **23**
Robin Hood La. *Winn* —2A **2**
Robin Hood Way. *Winn* —1A **2**
Robin La. *Sand* —2D **22**
Roby Dri. *Brack* —4D **14**
Rockfield Way. *Col T* —2F **23**
Roebuck Est. *Binf* —3E **5**
Rokeby Clo. *Brack* —4D **6**
Roman Ride. *Crowt* —3A **20**
Roman Way. *Warf* —4F **7**
Romeo Hill. *Warf* —4F **7**
Romney Ho. *Brack* —1E **15**
Romsey Clo. *B'water* —4E **23**
Rook Clo. *Wokgm* —1C **10**
Rookswood. *Brack* —3B **6**
Rookwood Av. *Owl* —6G **21**
Rosebay. *Wokgm* —4A **4**
Rose Ct. *Wokgm* —6G **3**
Rosedale. *Binf* —1E **5**
Rosedale Gdns. *Brack* —2A **14**
Rosedene La. *Col T* —4F **23**
Rose Gdns. *Wokgm* —6G **3**
Rose Hill. *Binf* —1E **5**
Rosemary Gdns. *B'water* —5E **23**
Rosemary La. *B'water* —4E **23**
Rose St. *Wokgm* —6G **3**
Rossett Clo. *Brack* —1B **14**
Rother Clo. *Sand* —2E **23**
Rotherfield Av. *Wokgm* —5D **2**
Rothwell Ho. *Crowt* —4E **21**
Roughgrove Copse. *Binf* —2D **4**
Roundabout La. *Winn* —4B **2**
Round Clo. *Yat* —5B **22**
Roundshead Dri. *Warf* —4D **6**
Rounds Hill. *Brack* —4G **5**
Rowan. *Brack* —2F **15**
Rowan Clo. *Wokgm* —1D **10**
Rowan Dri. *Crowt* —1E **21**
Rowley Clo. *Brack* —6E **7**
Royal Oak Clo. *Yat* —4A **22**
Royal Victoria Gdns. *S Asc* —1E **17**
Roycroft La. *Wokgm* —6C **10**
Ruby Clo. *Wokgm* —5B **2**
Rugby Clo. *Owl* —1G **23**
Ruskin Ct. *Crowt* —4A **20**
Ruskin Way. *Wokgm* —6B **2**
Russell Clo. *Brack* —5D **14**
Russell Ct. *B'water* —5F **23**
Russell Way. *Winn* —3A **2**
Russley Grn. *Wokgm* —5E **11**
Ruston Way. *Asc* —5C **8**
Ryan Mt. *Sand* —2C **22**
Rye Clo. *Brack* —3D **6**
Ryecroft Gdns. *B'water* —6G **23**

**S**adlers Ct. *Winn* —4B **2**
Sadlers End. *Sind* —5A **2**
Sadlers La. *Winn* —4B **2**
Saffron Rd. *Brack* —1B **14**
Sage Wlk. *Warf* —3D **6**
St Andrews. *Brack* —3G **13**
St Andrew's Clo. *Crowt* —2B **20**
St Annes Dri. *Wokgm* —6C **4**
St Anthonys Clo. *Brack* —4A **6**
St Christophers Gdns. *Asc* —4B **8**
St Georges Ct. *Owl* —6G **21**
St George's La. *Asc* —6F **9**
St Helens Cres. *Sand* —2D **22**
St Helier Clo. *Wokgm* —3F **11**
St James Rd. *Wokgm* —6C **10**
St John's Rd. *Asc* —3D **8**
St John's Rd. *Sand* —3D **22**
St Mark's Rd. *Binf* —3E **5**
St Mary's Clo. *Sand* —2E **23**
St Mary's Hill. *Asc* —3G **17**
St Mary's Rd. *Asc* —4F **17**
St Michael's Rd. *Sand* —2B **22**
St Paul's Ga. *Wokgm* —5E **3**
St Peter's Gdns. *Yat* —4A **22**
St Sebastian's Clo. *Wokgm* —1A **20**
Salamanca. *Crowt* —3A **20**
Sale Garden Cotts. *Wokgm* —1G **11**
Salisbury Clo. *Wokgm* —4E **11**
Salisbury Rd. *B'water* —6E **23**
Saltire Gdns. *Brack* —4A **6**
Salwey Clo. *Brack* —3B **14**
Samian Pl. *Binf* —3G **5**
Sampson Pk. *Binf* —4F **5**
Sandford Down. *Brack* —2F **15**
Sandhurst-Crowthorne By-Pass. *Crowt* —1G **21**
Sandhurst-Crowthorne By-Pass. *Sand* —5G **23**
Sandhurst La. *B'water* —4D **22**
Sandhurst Rd. *Crowt* —5D **20**
Sandhurst Rd. *Finch* —6F **11**
Sandhurst Rd. *Yat* —3B **22**
Sandown Clo. *B'water* —5F **23**
Sandstone Clo. *Winn* —3A **2**
Sandy La. *Brack* —4C **6**
Sandy La. *N Asc* —4A **8**
Sandy La. *Sand* —1B **22**
Sandy La. *S'dale* —2C **18**
Sandy La. *Wokgm* —2A **10**
Sandy Ride. *S'hill* —1A **18**
Sapphire Clo. *Wokgm* —5C **2**
Sarum. *Brack* —5H **13**
Sarum Cres. *Wokgm* —5H **3**
Saturn Clo. *Wokgm* —6C **2**
Saturn Croft. *Wink R* —2G **7**
Savernake Way. *Brack* —3E **15**